I0518374

The Dwelling Place

From Eden's Garden to the New Jerusalem

PUBLISHED BY: Ascend Life Publishing

The Dwelling Place

The Dwelling Place – From Eden's Garden to the New Jerusalem

© 2025 by Jed Brumfield

All rights reserved.

No part of this publication may be reproduced, stored in a retrieval system, or transmitted in any form or by any means—electronic, mechanical, photocopying, recording, or otherwise—without prior written permission of the publisher, except in the case of brief quotations used in critical articles and reviews.

Published by: Ascend Life Publishing

Baton Rouge, Louisiana

ISBN: 979-8-9932853-4-4

Unless otherwise noted, all Scripture quotations are taken from the English Standard Version (ESV) of the Bible, copyright © 2001 by Crossway, a publishing ministry of Good News Publishers. Used by permission. All rights reserved.

Additional Scripture quotations may appear from the New International Version (NIV), copyright © 1973, 1978, 1984, 2011 by Biblica, Inc.™ Used by permission. All rights reserved worldwide.

Dedication

To the enduring legacy of Dr. Myles Munroe, whose life and ministry awakened in me a profound understanding of the Kingdom of God. My ministerial journey began with a word about the Kingdom, and that word has become the foundation upon which every page of this book is built. Your passion for equipping believers to live as Kingdom citizens continues to inspire, challenge, and shape me.

Dr. Munroe's life was a testament to the power of vision, purpose, and faithful stewardship. His teachings ignited a passion in my heart to explore Scripture with fresh eyes, to embrace my calling with boldness, and to live every day with the understanding that the Kingdom of God is not just a distant hope but a present reality. Through his books, sermons, and personal example, Dr. Munroe taught countless people—including me—that leadership is not about status but service. That true greatness is found in submitting to the purposes of God.

This work is dedicated in gratitude to your example, teaching, and enduring influence, which continue to ripple through the global church. Though you have stepped into glory, your voice echoes still, calling a generation to rise up with Kingdom vision and Kingdom character. May this book, in some small way, carry forward the flame you lit and inspire others to take hold of their divine purpose, living for the glory of the King and the advancement of His Kingdom on earth as it is in heaven.

Acknowledgments

I am deeply grateful to those who have stood with me throughout this writing and spiritual reflection journey.
To my beloved wife, Sha'Myra Brumfield—your unwavering love, encouragement, and prayers have been my anchor, strength, and constant source of joy.
To my children, Caleb and Jaed—thank you for filling my life with joy, wonder, and purpose. I pray this work becomes part of your spiritual heritage.

I honor Dr. Johnny Young, Jr., whose prophetic insight and spiritual discernment first recognized God's pastoral calling upon my life. This work is a testament to the seed you have sown in me and the countless lives you have touched through your faithfulness and love for Christ.

I am also grateful to Elder Reggie Brumfield, Albert Davis Jr., Reggie Davis Sr., LeAnn Davis, Kedrick Simmons, Christy Simmons, Shantell Anderson, Eric Snowden, PJ Snowden, Dr. Stephen Johnson, and Dr. Ewell Netter. Your prayers, encouragement, and steadfast belief in me have been invaluable.

Finally, to all who have prayed, encouraged, and believed in the vision of this project—thank you. This book is the fruit of many hands, many prayers, and the grace of God, offered to His glory and for the edification of His people.

Preface

The story of Scripture is a story of presence. From the opening pages of Genesis, where God walked with humanity in the cool of the garden, to the closing vision in Revelation, where His dwelling is forever with His redeemed, the Bible reveals a single, unbroken theme: God's relentless desire to dwell with His people. This is not an incidental detail, but the heartbeat of the biblical narrative—the golden thread that unites creation, covenant, redemption, and consummation.

This book was born out of both study and pilgrimage. As a pastor, I have seen firsthand how God's presence sustains, transforms, and empowers His people in the ordinary rhythms of life and ministry. As a theologian and student of Scripture, I have been compelled to explore how deeply the theme of God's dwelling runs through the biblical canon and through the history of the Church. These pages represent the convergence of both callings—the academic pursuit of truth and the pastoral longing to shepherd others into deeper communion with the living God.

Throughout this journey, I have been shaped by the wisdom of those before me. The Church Fathers, Reformers, and modern theologians' voices remind us that God's presence is not an abstract concept, but a lived reality. The insights of teachers such as Myles Munroe, Tony Evans, Michael Bird, and others have been particularly formative for me, highlighting the Kingdom of God as both a present calling and a future hope. Their writings, coupled with my own experiences of prayer, worship, and leadership, have impressed upon me the urgency of reclaiming God's dwelling presence as central to our identity and mission.

This work is not intended to be merely a theological reflection or a practical instruction. It is meant to be both. Each chapter is written to draw readers into the grand biblical story while equipping them to live as participants in that story. I pray this book will serve pastors seeking to ground their congregations, students longing for theological clarity, and everyday believers desiring to know God more intimately.

Above all, this is an invitation. It is an invitation to recognize that God's dwelling place is not only a hope reserved for the future, but a present reality we are called to embody here and now. From Eden's garden to the wilderness tabernacle, from the incarnation of Christ to the indwelling Spirit, from the Church as God's temple to the eternal city of God, the story has always been about His nearness. Moreover, it is this nearness—this unbroken fellowship—that defines both our present calling and our eternal destiny.

As you turn these pages, may your mind be sharpened, your heart stirred, and your life reoriented around the God who has always longed to dwell with His people. May this work not only inform but inspire, not only explain but awaken, not only describe but call forth a deeper pursuit of the One who is our dwelling place—until that day when we shall see His face in the New Jerusalem.

Introduction

At the heart of Scripture lies one unshakable truth: God desires to dwell with His people. From the garden of Eden, where fellowship with the Creator was unbroken, to the New Jerusalem, where His presence will fill eternity, the Bible reveals a single, unifying theme—God's relentless pursuit of communion with humanity. This is the golden thread of redemptive history, the story that shapes our past, defines our present, and directs our future.

The purpose of this book is twofold. First, it seeks to demonstrate that the dwelling presence of God is not a minor theme but the central framework of the biblical canon. Every covenant, every act of redemption, and every movement of God's Spirit is aimed at restoring what was lost in Eden: intimacy between Creator and creation. Second, it aims to show how this reality shapes Christian identity, worship, discipleship, and mission in the world today. To speak of God's dwelling is not to deal with abstract theology, but with the very essence of what it means to be human in relationship with the divine.

This is a theological journey, but it is also a pastoral one. It engages Scripture carefully, listens to the wisdom of the Church through the ages, and draws insight from voices—ancient and modern—who have reminded us that the Kingdom of God is both a present reality and a future hope. However, this work was not written only for scholars. It is written for pastors seeking to shepherd their congregations, students longing for deeper understanding, and believers who desire to walk daily in God's presence. I pray that these pages will meet you wherever you are and draw you closer to the God who draws near.

The book is organized into four parts:

Part I Begins with Chapter 1- Foundations of God's Dwelling with His People: The Christian journey begins with communion. In this section, we explore how prayer, Scripture, worship, and gratitude serve as the foundational rhythms through which God's presence becomes real and transformative in the believer's daily life. These practices cultivate intimacy with the Lord and anchor us in His dwelling.

Part II Begins with Chapter 6- God's Presence Forming His People: God's dwelling is not static; His presence actively shapes His people. Here we turn to the themes of obedience, holiness, and the Spirit's indwelling, showing how God forms us into Christ's likeness. This section emphasizes that transformation is both a gift of grace and a call to faithfulness, as we learn to live as a holy people set apart for Him.

Part III Begins with Chapter 9- God's Presence in the Mission of the Kingdom: Communion with God is never meant to terminate on the individual. In this section, we discover how abiding in God leads to fruitful ministry, perseverance, and Kingdom impact. The mission of God flows from the presence of God, reminding us that authentic leadership and service come only from those who remain rooted in Christ.

Part IV Begins with Chapter 13- The Consummation of God's Dwelling: The biblical story culminates in God's eternal dwelling with His people. This final section lifts our eyes to the Garden restored in the New Jerusalem, where the river of life and the tree of healing point to the fullness of God's promise. Here, hope and anticipation fuel our present journey, as we prepare for the day when His presence will be our everlasting home.

The journey from Eden's garden to the eternal city is not merely a theological framework to be studied—it is the reality we live and the hope for which we long. I pray that this introduction will prepare your heart and mind to see the following pages as an invitation into that greater story. We are called not only to anticipate God's dwelling in the coming age, but to live even now as His dwelling place—temples of His Spirit, communities of His Kingdom, and witnesses of His presence in a world longing for redemption.

How to Use This Book

This book is written to serve a broad audience, and readers may approach it in different ways depending on their needs:

- **For personal devotion** – Read one chapter at a time, slowly reflecting on the Scripture references and theological insights. Use the questions and themes to guide prayer and journaling, allowing the message of God's dwelling to shape your daily walk with Him.

- **For pastors and ministry leaders** – Use the book as a preaching and teaching resource. Each part provides a theological foundation that can be translated into sermons, Bible studies, or discipleship courses designed to root congregations in the presence of God.

- **For theological students and scholars** – Read the book as a theological exploration of a canonical theme. Trace how the motif of God's dwelling unfolds across the biblical narrative, and engage with the scholarly sources cited for further study and research.

- **For small groups or communities** – Journey through the book together, discussing one chapter at a time. Reflect on how the truths about God's presence speak into shared life and mission.

No matter how you engage with it, the goal remains the same: to encounter God who dwells with His people and embody His presence in the world until His dwelling is complete.

The Dwelling Place

Chapter 1

Awaken Your Connection

Every journey toward spiritual maturity begins with a relationship—an intentional, sustained connection with God. While theology, doctrine, and ministry are critical elements of Christian growth, they are fruitless without the root of intimacy. The first step is not doing more for God but always being with Him. Before we learn to preach, lead, serve, or teach, we must learn to abide. This chapter sets the foundation for the spiritual journey by exploring the biblical, theological, and historical framework for cultivating daily communion with God.

Created for Connection

Scripture begins with connection. Humanity's creation in the image of God (Gen. 1:26–27) implies relational design. The triune God (Father, Son, and Holy Spirit) eternally exists in communion. To bear His image is to be made for relationship. Victor Hamilton explains, "The divine image endows humanity with a special status in creation, reflecting God's authority over the world"[1]. However, that image also implies our capacity for spiritual intimacy.

---

[1] Hamilton, Victor P. 1990. The Book of Genesis, Chapters 1–17. Grand Rapids: Eerdmans. Pg. 140

Genesis 3:8 offers a striking portrait of this reality: "And they heard the sound of the Lord God walking in the garden in the cool of the day." This daily rhythm of fellowship reflects the relational context of Eden. The regular, personal encounters Adam and Eve experienced with God signify the ideal state of human existence, living in conscious awareness and mutual interaction with the Creator. This communion was not limited to special occasions or rituals but permeated everyday life, establishing a pattern for humanity's intended experience.

However, this profound connection was profoundly disrupted with the entrance of sin. Shame and fear replaced openness and intimacy, compelling Adam and Eve to hide from the very presence they once cherished. Although the image of God within humanity was marred, it was not lost entirely. God, in His enduring mercy, began a divine initiative to reclaim and restore that original closeness. From this point forward, the Bible's narrative chronicles God's relentless pursuit to restore this relational chasm.

Throughout the Scriptures, God consistently initiates steps toward restoring communion with His creation. By calling Abraham to "walk before me and be blameless" (Gen. 17:1), God underscores that restored connection is possible through ongoing, faithful relationship rather than mere compliance with rules or regulations. Similarly, God's promise to Israel, "I will walk among you and be your God" (Lev. 26:12), demonstrates His unwavering commitment to presence and proximity, even amidst human imperfection.

The New Covenant vividly illustrates God's ultimate plan for relational restoration. Through the sacrificial work of Jesus Christ, not only was humanity's sin forgiven, but believers were given the indwelling presence of the Holy Spirit, permanently reestablishing the intimate connection first enjoyed in Eden. This indwelling presence—God living within us- marks the pinnacle of God's redemptive plan, offering believers continuous access to fellowship and intimacy with Him.

Biblical figures like Enoch and David provide powerful examples of lives characterized by ongoing intimacy with God. Enoch's relationship is described succinctly yet powerfully: "Enoch walked with God" (Gen. 5:24). This simple statement implies a lifetime of continuous, meaningful interaction and communion with God. Similarly, despite significant personal flaws, David's relationship with God is remembered primarily for its relational depth. He was known as "a man after God's own heart" (1 Sam. 13:14), a title highlighting his genuine pursuit and responsiveness to God's presence and will.

These examples illuminate what humanity was created for: continuous, authentic, and meaningful relationships with God. Our spiritual journey toward maturity begins by recognizing and embracing this foundational truth. Each day is an invitation to live in awareness of God's presence, walking in the original relational intimacy for which we were created.

Jesus and the Theology of Abiding

In the Gospels, Jesus embodies perfect communion with the Father. He rises early to pray (Mark 1:35), withdraws often (Luke 5:16), and testifies, "The Son can do nothing of his own accord, but only what he sees the Father doing" (John 5:19). This pattern is not incidental—it is central to His ministry and identity.

The lifestyle Jesus models is marked by intentional connection and ongoing intimacy. Throughout His earthly ministry, His consistent engagement in prayer and solitude provided clarity, guidance, and strength. His actions and teachings emerged directly from this intimate communion with the Father, demonstrating how abiding profoundly shapes a believer's life and ministry.

In John 15, Jesus uses the metaphor of the vine and branches: "Abide in me, and I in you. As the branch cannot bear fruit by itself... so neither can you unless you abide in me" (John 15:4, ESV). The Greek word for "abide" (menō) implies dwelling, remaining, and enduring. It is both a place and a posture. Augustine echoes this when he writes, "Our hearts are restless until they rest in Thee"[2]

Jesus invites all believers into this pattern of abiding. His high priestly prayer extends this relational intimacy beyond the original disciples, praying explicitly that future followers "may all be one... just as you, Father, are in me, and I in you" (John 17:21). This profound prayer illustrates Jesus' desire for all believers to experience profound, relational union with God.

The abiding life, therefore, involves deliberate spiritual disciplines such as prayer, meditation on Scripture, and intentional withdrawal for solitude, fostering an environment where intimacy can flourish. Through such disciplines, believers practically cultivate the abiding relationship modeled perfectly by Jesus.

---

[2] Augustine. [398] 1998. *Confessions*. Translated by Henry Chadwick. Oxford: Oxford University Press.

A Biblical Pattern of Daily Intimacy

The pattern of daily intimacy with God is evident throughout the Scriptures. From the consistent morning devotions depicted in the Psalms (Ps. 5:3) to Daniel's unwavering commitment to prayer three times a day (Dan. 6:10), the Bible consistently portrays intimacy with God as an ongoing, deliberate, daily pursuit. This practice of drawing near to God each day reveals not only a theological principle but a lived experience among the faithful.

The life of Jesus further reinforces this pattern. His early morning prayers (Mark 1:35), His retreat into solitude (Luke 5:16), and His engagement with the Father in moments of decision and distress demonstrate a life immersed in divine communion. This rhythm was not sporadic but essential to His spiritual vitality and mission.

In his letters, Paul emphasizes the importance of unceasing prayer and continuous communion with God. When he writes, "pray without ceasing" (1 Thess. 5:17), he is not suggesting endless verbal prayer, but rather a posture of the heart that remains aligned with and attentive to God throughout every activity of the day. This inner awareness becomes a spiritual compass, guiding thought, emotion, and action.

In the Old Testament, David models this pattern in his psalms, where he speaks of meditating on God day and night (Ps. 1:2; Ps. 119:97). His life, marked by triumph and failure, was consistently oriented toward God's presence. His words often reflect not just prayerful petition, but deep relational awareness—confession, praise, and reflection in the context of divine nearness.

Daily intimacy with God is not only done in moments of crisis or as a ritual obligation—it is designed to be the soul's natural habitat. The biblical witness is clear: those who walk closely with God do so intentionally, building rhythms of prayer, meditation, and worship into their daily lives. These rhythms do not constrain freedom; they enhance it by anchoring the heart in what is eternal.

For the believer today, this biblical pattern provides both invitation and instruction. Developing consistent engagement habits—beginning the day with prayer, immersing oneself in Scripture, practicing gratitude and silence—fosters a lifestyle of spiritual attentiveness. This attentiveness nurtures transformation, allowing believers to perform religious acts and become people shaped by divine presence.

True spiritual maturity is not found in the accumulation of knowledge or the perfection of performance, but in the consistency of communion. As the believer aligns more closely with this biblical pattern, they grow in their understanding of God and their likeness to Him.

This biblical pattern encourages believers today to cultivate habits that foster continuous awareness of God's presence—prayerful reflection, Scripture engagement, and intentional silence—allowing spiritual intimacy to become as natural and vital as breathing.

Historical Models of Communion

Church history is rich with examples of believers who prioritized intimacy with God. The early monastics, such as Antony of Egypt and John Cassian, withdrew into solitude not to escape the world but to seek God undistracted. Their rhythm of prayer and labor gave rise to the Benedictine Rule, which balanced ora et labora—prayer and work.[3]

Medieval mystics like Julian of Norwich and Teresa of Ávila emphasized interior union with Christ. Teresa's *Interior Castle* presents the soul as a mansion with many rooms, the innermost being the place of divine communion.[4]

Though reacting against monasticism abuses, the Reformers retained a high view of daily devotion. Martin Luther famously said, "I have so much to do that I shall spend the first three hours in prayer." John Calvin emphasized "true piety" as a sincere reverence toward God that touches all of life.[5]

In the modern era, Brother Lawrence's *The Practice of the Presence of God* has been a manual for living daily in God's nearness. He writes, "The time of business does not with me differ from the time of prayer."[6] Frank Laubach, a missionary in the 20th century, practiced "game with minutes," attempting to bring God to mind each minute of the day.

Barriers to Connection in a Distracted Age

While divine presence is always available, the human capacity to dwell in that presence has become increasingly fragile in modern society. We live in a culture saturated with

---

[3] Benedict. [c. 540] 1981. *The Rule of St. Benedict.* Collegeville, MN: Liturgical Press.
[4] Teresa of Ávila. [1577] 1961. *The Interior Castle.* Translated by E. Allison Peers. Garden City, NY: Doubleday
[5] Calvin, John. [1559] 2008. *Institutes of the Christian Religion.* Translated by Henry Beveridge. Peabody, MA: Hendrickson Publishers
[6] Lawrence, Brother. [1692] 2005. *The Practice of the Presence of God.* Mineola, NY: Dover Publications

distractions, constant notifications, infinite digital noise, and an ever-accelerating pace of life. These forces, though subtle, can dull our spiritual senses and erode our attentiveness to God.

One of the greatest threats to spiritual connection in the modern age is the fragmentation of attention. The average person today is overwhelmed with more information in a single day than a person in the Middle Ages would encounter in a year. Social media, streaming platforms, and relentless news cycles condition our minds toward constant stimulation and reactive thinking. In this environment, the stillness required for intimacy with God becomes rare and difficult to tolerate.

Another barrier is the tyranny of busyness. Even within ministry and church culture, activity is often mistaken for intimacy. It is possible to serve God publicly while remaining distant from Him privately. The calendar can become full, while the soul remains empty. Jesus warned Martha of this tendency when He said, "You are anxious and troubled about many things, but one thing is necessary" (Luke 10:41–42, ESV). Mary chose presence over performance—and Jesus commended her for it.

In addition to distraction and busyness, secularism poses a more existential barrier. In a world that increasingly views spiritual life as optional or irrational, believers often internalize the cultural pressure to compartmentalize faith. God becomes reserved for Sunday mornings or crisis moments, rather than remaining the focal point of everyday life. This compartmentalization suffocates spiritual vitality. Charles Taylor refers to this cultural framework as the "immanent frame," a view of the world where transcendence is excluded by default.[7]

Lastly, emotional and spiritual fatigue, often the result of burnout, unresolved trauma, or chronic stress, can cloud our ability to connect with God. We may believe in His love intellectually, yet feel disconnected from it experientially. The Psalms are honest about these seasons: "How long, O Lord? Will you forget me forever?" (Ps. 13:1, ESV). These moments invite not shame, but surrender.

Overcoming these barriers requires more than willpower; it requires formation. Believers must reorder their lives around practices that slow the soul, quiet the noise, and create space for God's presence to be recognized again. As Dallas Willard puts it, "Hurry is the great enemy of spiritual life in our day. You must ruthlessly eliminate hurry from your life."[8] This is not retreating from reality; it is recovering the true center of it.

---

[7] Taylor, Charles. 2007. *A Secular Age*. Cambridge, MA: Harvard University Press

[8] Willard, Dallas. 1998. *The Spirit of the Disciplines*. San Francisco: HarperOne

Spiritual Habits That Cultivate Intimacy

Restored connection often begins with rhythms—daily choices that create space for encounter. Richard Foster writes, "The spiritual disciplines are the means by which we place ourselves where God can bless us."[9]

- **Prayer**: Both structured (like the Lord's Prayer) and spontaneous, prayer keeps the soul open to God.

- **Scripture meditation**: Not merely reading but listening, reflecting, and responding (Ps. 1:2).

- **Silence and solitude**: In stillness, we learn to discern God's voice (Ps. 46:10).

- **Confession**: Regular self-examination clears relational clutter (1 John 1:9).

- **Gratitude**: Giving thanks aligns the heart with God's goodness (1 Thess. 5:18).

Classical practices like *lectio divina* (sacred reading), the *daily examen* (prayerful reflection), and keeping a *rule of life* offer structure without rigidity. These tools cultivate attentiveness, deepen receptivity, and nurture the soul's capacity for God.

The Spirit's Role in Sustaining Connection

True intimacy with God is not achieved by human effort alone—it is initiated, sustained, and empowered by the Holy Spirit. Jesus described the Spirit as the Helper, the One who would come to dwell in believers and guide them into all truth

---

[9] Foster, Richard. 1978. *Celebration of Discipline: The Path to Spiritual Growth*. San Francisco: Harper & Row

(John 14:26). This divine indwelling is not merely a theological theory; it is the ongoing source of life, wisdom, conviction, and comfort in the believer's daily walk.

Paul speaks to this reality when he describes believers as "temples of the Holy Spirit" (1 Cor. 6:19). This imagery underscores the nearness of God—not as one who visits occasionally, but as one who takes up permanent residence within. The Spirit is not an accessory to the Christian life; He is essential to every dimension.

One of the Spirit's roles is to empower communion with God in both word and silence. Paul writes that "the Spirit helps us in our weakness" and "intercedes for us with groanings too deep for words" (Rom. 8:26, ESV). This means that the Spirit bridges the gap even when the believer is too weary, confused, or broken to articulate prayers. Intimacy is maintained not by eloquence, but by presence—His presence.

The Spirit also fosters sensitivity. What begins as a whisper becomes a pattern of prompting, conviction, encouragement, or redirection. He speaks through Scripture, nudges the heart toward repentance, and comforts in seasons of sorrow. The more one learns to listen, the more one discovers the Spirit's faithful companionship.

Moreover, the Spirit strengthens the believer to persevere in spiritual practices. Prayer, worship, and study are not meant to be sustained by human discipline alone. The Spirit infuses them with life. He turns duty into delight. He transforms silence into sacred space. He makes the Word come alive.

J.I. Packer captures this truth beautifully, who writes, "The Christian's life in all its aspects—intellectual and ethical, devotional and relational, upsurging in worship and outgoing in witness—is supernatural."[10]

Conclusion: Returning to the Center

Awakening your connection with God is not a peripheral matter; it is the core of all other spiritual growth. Ministry, mission, and maturity are fruitless without abiding. As Jesus said, "Apart from me, you can do nothing" (John 15:5).

This first habit is not about adding more to your schedule but reprioritizing your soul. It is about saying "yes" to the original design and deepest longing: to walk with God. The invitation remains in a world that pulls us in every direction: Draw near. Abide. Be still. Listen. Respond.

This is where the journey begins.

---

[10] Packer, J.I. 1993. *Knowing God.* Downers Grove, IL: InterVarsity Press

Chapter 2

Plant the Word Deeply – Scripture as the Soil of Spiritual Transformation

Scripture is not simply a text to be read; it is a living Word to be planted, nurtured, and cultivated until it bears the fruit of spiritual transformation. The call to plant the Word deeply is urgent and timeless in a world of many distractions and surface-level encounters. It is a call to move beyond casual reading and into a rhythm of intentional, sustained engagement with the divine revelation of God.

This chapter explores the multifaceted process of planting the Word within the heart, drawing from biblical, historical, and contemporary perspectives to provide a comprehensive framework for internalizing Scripture. More than an academic exercise, it is a spiritual discipline that demands focus, patience, and a willingness to be transformed from the inside out. If spiritual intimacy is the root of growth, Scripture is the soil where transformation takes root and flourishes. A deep and abiding relationship with the Word of God is central to every phase of the believer's journey. More than just information, Scripture is revelation—God's voice revealed and preserved across centuries, shaping the lives of those who allow it to dwell richly within them.[11] In this chapter, we explore the theological, biblical, historical, and practical dimensions of planting the Word deeply, anchoring the soul in truth that forms, reforms, and conforms us into the image of Christ.

The Word as Seed: Biblical Foundations

The metaphor of the Word as seed is one of the most powerful and recurring images in Scripture. Jesus masterfully uses this imagery in the Parable of the Sower (Matt. 13:1–9, 18–23), emphasizing that the Word of God, like seed, carries the potential for life, growth, and transformation. However, its impact is determined by the soil—the heart of the hearer. The same seed that produces abundant fruit in one person may be snatched away, choked, or scorched in another, revealing that the power of the Word is not limited but that the receptivity of the heart plays a crucial role in its effectiveness.[12]

Isaiah further illustrates this principle, declaring, "As the rain and the snow come down from heaven and do not return to it without watering the earth and making it bud and flourish... so is my word that goes out from my mouth; it will not return to me empty" (Isa. 55:10–11, ESV). Just as rain and snow saturate the ground, preparing it to bring forth life, so the Word saturates the soul, preparing it to bear spiritual fruit. The imagery is not passive but active; God's Word accomplishes what He intends, but only when planted and nurtured over time.

---

[11] Willard, Dallas. 1998. *The Spirit of the Disciplines: Understanding How God Changes Lives*. San Francisco: HarperSanFrancisco

[12] Calvin, John. [1559] 2008. *Institutes of the Christian Religion*. Translated by Henry Beveridge. Peabody, MA: Hendrickson Publishers

Throughout the Old Testament, the concept of planting and sowing is closely connected to the idea of spiritual cultivation. The prophet Hosea urges, "Sow righteousness for yourselves, reap the fruit of unfailing love, and break up your unplowed ground" (Hos. 10:12, ESV). Here, the call to break up fallow ground implies that the heart can become hardened, resistant, or distracted. The Word cannot take root in a hardened heart any more than seed can grow in unbroken soil.

David's psalms reinforce the necessity of planting the Word deeply. He describes the righteous as "a tree planted by streams of water, which yields its fruit in season and whose leaf does not wither" (Ps. 1:3, ESV). The key to this flourishing is not effort but delight in the law of the Lord, meditating on it day and night (Ps. 1:2). The word "meditate" here, from the Hebrew *hagah*, conveys the sense of murmuring, pondering, and deeply absorbing the Word until it becomes part of the inner life.[13]

In the New Testament, Paul builds upon this agricultural imagery, asserting that "whatever one sows, that will he also reap" (Gal. 6:7, ESV). The apostle's exhortation underscores the inevitability of spiritual harvest—whether good or bad. Planting the Word deeply means intentionally sowing seeds of truth, righteousness, and obedience, with the understanding that the harvest will come in due time. Thus, planting is not a one-time act but a continual process of sowing, watering, weeding, and waiting.

Moreover, the seed metaphor suggests that the Word, once planted, has inherent life-giving power. Peter writes, "You

---

[13] Luther, Martin. 1966. *Luther's Works, Vol. 35: Word and Sacrament I.* Edited by E. Theodore Bachmann. Philadelphia: Fortress Press

have been born again, not of perishable seed but of imperishable, through God's living and abiding word" (1 Pet. 1:23, ESV). This imperishable seed is the gospel—the ultimate Word that has the power to regenerate, renew, and transform.

Planting the Word is not simply about absorbing information but cultivating a life that becomes fertile ground for divine truth. The believer is called to not only hear the Word but to hold onto it, guard it, and nurture it, allowing it to penetrate deeply into the heart and bear lasting fruit (John 15:7).

Jesus taught that the Word of God is like seed—alive, full of potential, yet dependent on the heart's receptivity (Matt. 13:1–9, 18–23). In the Parable of the Sower, He illustrated four types of soil representing four types of hearers. The seed remains the same; the condition of the ground differs. Transformation is not limited by the power of the Word but by the posture of the recipient.[14]

The imagery of the seed captures the essential nature of Scripture. The Word must be planted, nurtured, and protected like a seed. It does not instantly bear fruit, but over time, it produces a harvest of righteousness in those who persevere. Isaiah affirms the power of God's Word: "so shall my word be that goes out from my mouth; it shall not return to me empty, but it shall accomplish that which I purpose" (Isa. 55:11, ESV). The Word does not fail, but its work is gradual, deep, and enduring.

Throughout Scripture, the metaphor of spiritual planting appears consistently. Psalm 1 compares the righteous to a tree planted by streams of water, whose leaf does not wither. The key

---

[14] Calvin, John. [1559] 2008. *Institutes of the Christian Religion*. Translated by Henry Beveridge. Peabody, MA: Hendrickson Publishers

to this vitality is that "his delight is in the law of the Lord, and on his law he meditates day and night" (Ps. 1:2–3, ESV). The imagery ties fruitfulness not to activity, but to rootedness in God's revelation (Luther 1966, 286).

Meditation and Internalization in Scripture

To plant the Word deeply is to move beyond surface reading and toward internalization. In Hebrew, the word for meditation, *hagah*, conveys a sense of murmuring, muttering, and pondering deeply.[15] It is not a passive act but an intentional, repetitive engagement with God's Word until it penetrates the heart and shapes the mind. Biblical meditation is distinct from emptying the mind; instead, it fills the mind with divine truth.

Joshua was instructed to meditate on the Law "day and night," a command that highlights the importance of continuous engagement with Scripture (Josh. 1:8). The purpose was not merely academic but transformational—to be careful to do all that was written in it. This meditation was not a one-time practice but a daily discipline, a rhythm that shaped Joshua's actions and decisions.

David, the psalmist, exemplifies this form of meditation. In Psalm 119, he declares, "Oh, how I love your law! It is my meditation all the day" (Ps. 119:97, ESV). For David, the Word of God was not a distant text but a living, breathing reality that provided counsel, comfort, and correction. His meditation was an act of drawing near, a continual return to the truths of God that anchored his soul.

---

[15] Bonhoeffer, Dietrich. 1954. *Life Together*. Translated by John W. Doberstein. New York: Harper & Row.

Internalization is the progression from reading to reflecting, from reflecting to remembering, and from remembering to embodying. When the Word becomes hidden in the heart (Ps. 119:11), it becomes readily accessible in moments of temptation, discouragement, or decision. Jesus demonstrated this principle in the wilderness when He responded to Satan, "It is written" (Matt. 4:4, 7, 10). His responses were not spontaneous but resulted from deep internalization of the Scriptures.[16]

The New Testament also emphasizes the transformative power of internalizing Scripture. Paul writes, "Let the word of Christ dwell in you richly, teaching and admonishing one another in all wisdom" (Col. 3:16, ESV). The verb "dwell" implies a continual, ongoing presence of the Word within the believer. It is not a fleeting encounter but a sustained residence, a permanent deposit that shapes thoughts, actions, and attitudes.

In the early church, internalization was practiced through *lectio divina*, a contemplative reading of Scripture involving reading, meditation, prayer, and contemplation. This practice, championed by the monastics and later formalized by Benedict, emphasized the slow, prayerful absorption of Scripture. The goal was not information but transformation—the cultivation of a mind steeped in the language and rhythms of the Word.[17]

In modern practice, internalization can take many forms: journaling, Scripture memorization, reflective reading, and silent meditation. The objective is not to master the text but to be mastered by it, allowing the Word to sink deeply, take root, and

---

[16] Taylor, Charles. 2007. *A Secular Age*. Cambridge, MA: Harvard University Press

[17] Origen. 1973. *Origen: An Exhortation to Martyrdom, Prayer, and Selected Works*. Translated by Rowan A. Greer. New York: Paulist Press.

bear fruit. When believers consistently meditate on Scripture, they align their minds with the mind of Christ, becoming living epistles that reflect the heart and character of God. Joshua was told to meditate on the Book of the Law "day and night," so he would carefully do everything written in it (Josh. 1:8).

This promise—prosperity and success—is not about worldly gain but spiritual stability. David echoed this theme throughout the Psalms: "Oh how I love your law! It is my meditation all the day" (Ps. 119:97). His passion for God's Word was not academic but intimate. The Word was his counselor, his comforter, his joy.

Internalization is the movement from reading to remembering to embodying. When the Word becomes hidden in the heart (Ps. 119:11), it becomes available in the moments we need it most—when facing temptation, discouragement, or decision. The Spirit brings to remembrance what has been stored within (John 14:26), but nothing that was never first implanted can be recalled.

Jesus and the Written Word

Jesus, the Living Word, honored and used the Written Word. His knowledge of Scripture was not simply doctrinal—it was personal, deeply internalized, and applied with precision. Jesus consistently referenced Scripture throughout His ministry as the ultimate authority, grounding His teachings, responses, and actions in the sacred text.

In the wilderness temptation (Matt. 4:1–11), Jesus did not wield supernatural power to defeat Satan but relied solely on Scripture. "It is written," He declared, not once but three times. Each time, He quoted Deuteronomy, a text given to Israel during their own wilderness testing. By anchoring His responses in Scripture, Jesus demonstrated that the Word is not merely a tool but a weapon against spiritual attack, a source of divine strength, and a revelation of God's character.[18]

Jesus' use of Scripture was not limited to conflict. He routinely read, interpreted, and fulfilled the Word in His public ministry. In the synagogue of Nazareth, He unrolled the scroll of Isaiah and proclaimed, "Today this Scripture has been fulfilled in your hearing" (Luke 4:21). In that moment, He identified Himself as the fulfillment of prophetic promise, positioning Scripture not as a historical document but as a living testament to the redemptive work of God.

Furthermore, Jesus affirmed the authority and permanence of Scripture: "Heaven and earth will pass away, but my words will not pass away" (Matt. 24:35, ESV). This declaration underscores the enduring relevance of Scripture, even as cultural norms and human traditions shift. For Jesus, the Word was immutable, eternal, and entirely trustworthy.

His reverence for Scripture extended to the most minor details. In Matthew 5:18, He stated that "not an iota, not a dot" would pass from the Law until all was accomplished. This meticulous respect for the written Word reflects the Jewish tradition of safeguarding every letter of the Torah. Jesus upheld Scripture as divinely inspired, precise, and authoritative, treating it as the very breath of God (2 Tim. 3:16).

Moreover, Jesus did not merely quote Scripture; He lived it. His actions embodied the prophetic texts He cited. When He

---

[18] Taylor, Charles. 2007. *A Secular Age*. Cambridge, MA: Harvard University Press

cleansed the temple, He declared, "My house shall be called a house of prayer" (Matt. 21:13), referencing Isaiah 56:7 and Jeremiah 7:11. In doing so, He enacted the very words He spoke, demonstrating that Scripture was not just to be read but incarnated.

In His final moments, Jesus continued to speak Scripture. On the cross, He cried, "My God, my God, why have you forsaken me?" (Matt. 27:46), quoting Psalm 22. This profound identification with the suffering psalmist reveals that Jesus clung to the Word even in agony. The Word was His anchor, sustenance, and ultimate declaration of trust in the Father.

Thus, to plant the Word deeply is to follow the example of Jesus—not just to read it, but to internalize it, live it, and wield it in every circumstance. Scripture was more than a text for Jesus; it was the lens through which He viewed every aspect of life, ministry, and mission. In the same way, believers are called to make Scripture their compass, their counsel, and their constant companion.

Historical Perspectives on Scripture Saturation

The role of Scripture in spiritual formation has been a central theme throughout church history. From the early Church Fathers to the Reformers and beyond, immersion in the Word of God was essential to spiritual growth, transformation, and cultivating a Christ-centered life. Each era, marked by unique challenges and theological emphases, demonstrates how deeply the Church has valued Scripture as both the source and sustenance of the believer's spiritual life.

In the early centuries of Christianity, figures such as Origen, Athanasius, and Augustine emphasized Scripture as text and encounter. Origen viewed the Bible as a multi-layered revelation containing literal, moral, and spiritual meanings, each uncovering deeper layers of divine truth.[19] His approach was not academic but devotional, encouraging believers to allow Scripture to penetrate and transform the heart.

In his Festal Letters, Athanasius underscored the necessity of daily Scripture reading. He continually instructed the faithful to meditate on the Psalms, asserting that they provided a complete spiritual guide for prayer, worship, and personal formation. For Athanasius, the Psalms were more than poetic expressions; they were spiritual nourishment, a divine curriculum for the soul.

Augustine, whose *Confessions* remains a seminal work on spiritual formation, spoke of Scripture as a mirror that reveals both the self and the Savior. He described the Word as the means by which God illuminates the darkened heart, leading the sinner to repentance and the saint to sanctification. Augustine's conversion narrative, marked by hearing a child chant, "Take up and read," exemplifies how the Word becomes a direct, personal call to spiritual awakening.

In the monastic tradition, the Rule of St. Benedict emphasized daily immersion in Scripture through the practice of *lectio divina*—a contemplative reading of the Word involving reading (*lectio*), meditation (*meditatio*), prayer (*oratio*), and contemplation (*contemplatio*). This rhythm of prayerful reading was not intended to produce scholars but saints, men and women whose lives were steeped in the Word. Benedictine monks would

---

[19] Origen. 1973. *Origen: An Exhortation to Martyrdom, Prayer, and Selected Works*. Translated by Rowan A. Greer. New York: Paulist Press

spend hours each day chanting, memorizing, and reflecting upon Scripture, allowing it to shape their inner lives and outward conduct.

During the Reformation, Martin Luther and John Calvin reinstated the primacy of Scripture as the foundation of Christian faith and practice. Luther, a former monk, famously declared, "Let the man who would hear God speak, read Holy Scripture."[20] He viewed the Bible as the final authority for faith and life, and his translation of the Scriptures into the vernacular opened the Word to ordinary people, making it accessible and transformative.

In his Institutes of the Christian Religion, John Calvin argued that the Word of God is the instrument by which the Holy Spirit works faith and renewal in the believer's heart.[21] He emphasized that knowledge of God is not gained through speculative theology but through immersion in the revealed Word. For Calvin, Scripture was not merely a historical document but the living voice of God, echoing through the ages and speaking to every generation.

In the modern era, figures such as Dietrich Bonhoeffer and Dallas Willard continued to emphasize the formative power of Scripture. In his communal experiment at Finkenwalde, Bonhoeffer required his students to meditate on a single verse of Scripture each morning, carrying it with them throughout the

---

[20] Luther, Martin. 1966. *Luther's Works, Vol. 35: Word and Sacrament I.* Edited by E. Theodore Bachmann. Philadelphia: Fortress Press
[21] Calvin, John. [1559] 2008. *Institutes of the Christian Religion.* Translated by Henry Beveridge. Peabody, MA: Hendrickson Publishers

day.[22] This practice of continuous reflection on the Word was intended to cultivate a life rooted in God's presence and governed by divine truth.

In his writings on spiritual disciplines, Willard underscored the necessity of Scripture saturation in a distracted age. He warned against the superficial engagement with Scripture that characterizes much of modern Christianity, urging believers to go beyond mere reading to a life where the Word "dwells richly" within, forming thoughts, actions, and desires.[23]

Thus, the historical emphasis on Scripture saturation reveals a consistent pattern: spiritual giants across centuries did not merely read the Word—they absorbed it, pondered it, and allowed it to transform them from the inside out. This historical legacy calls modern believers to do the same, making Scripture a study and a way of life.

Modern Challenges to Scripture Engagement

Despite the unprecedented availability of Scripture in the modern world, biblical engagement has reached a historic low. The rise of digital distractions, shifting cultural values, and theological relativism has contributed to widespread spiritual malnourishment. While believers have access to multiple translations, study tools, and Bible apps, the depth of interaction with the Word has often been reduced to brief, surface-level

---

[22] Bonhoeffer, Dietrich. 1954. *Life Together*. Translated by John W. Doberstein. New York: Harper & Row.
[23] Willard, Dallas. 1998. *The Spirit of the Disciplines: Understanding How God Changes Lives*. San Francisco: HarperSanFrancisco

encounters rather than sustained, transformative engagement.[24](Willard 1998, 42).

One of the most pervasive challenges is the culture of distraction. Constant notifications, endless scrolling, and rapid information consumption characterize the digital age. The average person now interacts with over 10,000 digital messages daily. This barrage of stimuli fragments attention, making it increasingly challenging to engage deeply with Scripture. The psalmist declared, "Be still, and know that I am God" (Ps. 46:10, ESV), but modern believers struggle to find such stillness amidst the noise.

Additionally, the secularization of society has contributed to the decline in Scripture engagement. Charles Taylor identifies this as the "immanent frame," a cultural framework in which spiritual realities are either marginalized or dismissed altogether.[25] As secularism redefines truth as relative and personal rather than absolute and divine, Scripture is increasingly perceived as outdated or irrelevant. This cultural shift has led many to approach the Bible not as authoritative revelation but as one voice among many, subject to personal interpretation.

Another challenge is the rise of pragmatism in spiritual practices. In a results-driven society, believers may approach Scripture as a quick fix for immediate concerns rather than a lifelong source of spiritual formation. Instead of seeking to be shaped by the Word, they seek to extract a verse to fit their

---

[24] Willard, Dallas. 1998. *The Spirit of the Disciplines: Understanding How God Changes Lives.* San Francisco: HarperSanFrancisco
[25] Taylor, Charles. 2007. *A Secular Age.* Cambridge, MA: Harvard University Press

situation. This consumer-oriented approach to Scripture neglects the transformative process of meditating on and internalizing the Word, reducing it to a collection of inspirational quotes rather than a comprehensive, life-altering revelation.

Moreover, theological relativism poses a significant threat to deep Scripture engagement. In an era where personal experience is often elevated above biblical authority, many believers reinterpret Scripture through the lens of cultural norms rather than allowing Scripture to interpret their experiences. This has led to selective reading, where challenging passages are either ignored or redefined to align with personal preferences, undermining the integrity and transformative power of the Word.

Lastly, emotional and spiritual fatigue can hinder Scripture engagement. Many believers are weary and overwhelmed in a world marked by constant crisis and uncertainty. They may desire to engage with Scripture but feel too mentally and emotionally depleted to focus on sustained reading or meditation. However, it is precisely in these moments that Scripture offers its greatest comfort and strength. The psalmist declares, "My soul clings to the dust; give me life according to your word" (Ps. 119:25, ESV). The Word is not merely a source of instruction—it is a source of renewal and life.

Addressing these modern challenges requires intentional, countercultural practices. It demands creating sacred spaces for undistracted Scripture reading, committing to biblical literacy in a culture of superficiality, and reclaiming the authority of God's Word in a world of competing narratives. Only then can believers move beyond shallow encounters with Scripture and enter into a transformative, abiding relationship with the Word.

Practical Habits for Planting the Word Deeply

Planting the Word deeply requires intentional habits. These are not rigid laws, but rhythms of grace that create space for the Spirit to work through Scripture.

1. **Daily Reading**: Establish a consistent time and place. Begin with prayer, asking the Spirit to illuminate the Word. Read slowly and attentively.

2. **Lectio Divina**: Engage Scripture with depth. Read the passage multiple times, listen for a word or phrase that stands out, reflect prayerfully, respond from the heart, and rest in God's presence.

3. **Scripture Memorization**: Commit key verses to memory. Review them daily. Carry them into your routines. Let them form your inner vocabulary.

4. **Journaling**: Write reflections, questions, and responses to Scripture. This practice helps track spiritual growth and records God's voice in your life.

5. **Scripture-Saturated Prayer**: Use the words of Scripture to guide your prayers. Let the Psalms become your petitions, praises, and laments.

6. **Community Engagement**: Read and discuss Scripture with others. Group study sharpens understanding and helps guard against private distortion.

These habits are not boxes to check but tools for transformation. As they are practiced over time, the Word takes root, bearing fruit in every season.

Conclusion: Becoming Living Epistles

The transformative power of Scripture is not found in merely reading its words but in allowing those words to take root, grow, and bear fruit in the soil of the heart. The believer who plants the Word deeply becomes a living epistle—a walking testimony to God's Word's life-giving, renewing power. Paul declared, "You are our letter, written on our hearts, known and read by everyone" (2 Cor. 3:2–3, ESV). To become such a letter, the Word must dwell richly within, saturating every thought, action, and motive.

In a world filled with noise and distraction, the planted Word becomes an anchor, holding the soul steady in times of trial and temptation. It provides clarity when confusion arises, strength when faith wavers, and conviction when compromise threatens. However, this transformative work requires intentionality—it demands that the believer not only read but meditate, not only memorize but internalize, not only hear but obey.

As the Word is planted, it gradually transforms the believer into the very image of Christ, producing a harvest of righteousness that endures in every season (James 1:21). Thus, planting the Word deeply is not a one-time act but a lifelong practice—a daily choice to let the Word of God take root, grow strong, and bear fruit that remains. Paul described the Corinthian believers as "a letter from Christ... written not with ink but with the Spirit of the living God, not on tablets of stone but on tablets of human hearts" (2 Cor. 3:3, ESV). This is the goal of planting the Word deeply: that we might become living epistles—embodied reflections of divine truth.[26]

When the Word dwells richly in us, it reshapes how we think, feel, speak, and live. It guards against deception, strengthens faith, fuels obedience, and equips us for every good work. It becomes the lamp to our feet and the light to our path (Ps. 119:105). In an age of noise and confusion, the planted Word offers clarity. In a culture of change and compromise, it offers constancy. In a world of despair, it offers hope.

---

[26] Bonhoeffer, Dietrich. 1954. *Life Together*. Translated by John W. Doberstein. New York: Harper & Row.

The Dwelling Place

Chapter 3

Strengthen the Line of Prayer — Developing Consistent and Powerful Communication with God

Prayer is the lifeline of the believer, a spiritual channel that connects the human soul to the divine presence of God. It is more than a ritual or religious obligation—it is a dynamic, ongoing conversation that fosters intimacy, builds faith, and aligns the heart with the will of God. However, developing a consistent and powerful prayer life requires intentional practice, theological understanding, and spiritual discipline in a world filled with distractions and noise. This chapter explores the transformative power of prayer, examining its biblical foundations, historical significance, and practical applications in the believer's daily life.

The Theology of Prayer: Understanding the Divine Connection

Prayer is not simply a monologue; it is a dialogue initiated by God. From the opening chapters of Genesis, we see that God desires communication with humanity. When Adam and Eve hid in the Garden, God called out, "Where are you?" (Gen. 3:9, ESV), initiating a pattern of divine pursuit throughout

Scripture. Prayer is not about informing God of our needs but aligning ourselves with His presence and purposes.[27]

Theologically, prayer is rooted in God as a relational being. Throughout the Old Testament, we encounter a God who speaks, listens, and responds to His people. The psalmist declared, "The Lord is near to all who call on him, to all who call on him in truth" (Ps. 145:18, ESV). This divine responsiveness reveals God's willingness to engage in intimate dialogue with humanity, a pattern fulfilled and intensified in the New Testament through Jesus Christ.

Jesus' teachings on prayer reveal its nature as both intimate and reverent. When asked how to pray, He provided the Lord's Prayer (Matt. 6:9–13), a model that balances adoration, petition, confession, and submission to God's will. This prayer structure directs our words and shapes our hearts, moving us from self-centered requests to God-centered communion. It is a framework for aligning earthly desires with heavenly purposes and participating in God's redemptive work on earth.[28] (Willard 1998).

Furthermore, prayer is a practice and a posture of the heart. Paul's epistles emphasize the necessity of persistent prayer. "Pray without ceasing," he writes (1 Thess. 5:17, ESV), urging believers to be continuously aware of God's presence. This call to constant prayer is not about endless verbal repetition

---

[27] Bonhoeffer, Dietrich. 1954. *Life Together.* Translated by John W. Doberstein. New York: Harper & Row
[28] Willard, Dallas. 1998. *The Spirit of the Disciplines: Understanding How God Changes Lives.* San Francisco: Harper, San Francisco

but cultivating a posture of spiritual attentiveness, allowing every thought, action, and word to be offered as a form of prayer.

Prayer also serves as a spiritual battleground. In Ephesians 6:18, Paul commands believers to "pray at all times in the Spirit, with all prayer and supplication." Here, prayer is positioned as a weapon in spiritual warfare, a means of accessing divine power to stand firm against the enemy's schemes. The intercessory nature of prayer involves seeking God's intervention for personal needs and standing in the gap for others, aligning with God's will for nations, communities, and individuals.

Theologically, prayer is an expression of faith and dependence on God. Calvin writes, "Prayer is the chief exercise of faith by which we daily receive God's benefits."[29] This perspective underscores that prayer is not a transactional activity but a relational act of trust, demonstrating our reliance on God's wisdom, provision, and timing.

Thus, prayer is far more than a religious duty—it is a dynamic, ongoing conversation with the Creator. It is the means by which the believer not only communes with God but also participates in unfolding His divine purposes. In this sense, prayer is the bridge between heaven and earth, a spiritual practice that roots the believer in God's presence and propels them forward in His mission.

---

[29] Calvin, John. [1559] 2008. *Institutes of the Christian Religion*. Translated by Henry Beveridge. Peabody, MA: Hendrickson Publishers

The Power of Prayer in Scripture

Throughout Scripture, prayer is depicted as a powerful force that moves heaven and earth. The prophets, patriarchs, and apostles relied on prayer to access divine intervention, seek guidance, and express worship. Prayer is portrayed not merely as a religious practice but as a spiritual weapon, a means by which believers align themselves with God's will and invite His intervention in earthly affairs.

In the Old Testament, we see Moses interceding for the Israelites, standing "in the gap" to avert God's wrath (Exod. 32:11–14). This intercession act demonstrates prayer's power to alter circumstances, change divine outcomes, and restore covenant relationships. Moses' prayer was not passive but fervent, faith-filled, and based on God's revealed character and promises. His intercession highlights the role of prayer as a form of spiritual advocacy, invoking God's mercy on behalf of others.

Similarly, Hannah's prayer for a child (1 Sam. 1:10–20) exemplifies the transformative power of persistent, faith-driven prayer. Her prayers were characterized by both intensity and vulnerability. She poured out her soul to God, refusing to be consoled until she received a response. Hannah's prayer was answered with Samuel's birth and became a prophetic declaration of God's faithfulness, a living testimony of God's power to turn barrenness into fruitfulness.

Elijah, the prophet, also demonstrated the miraculous power of prayer in his confrontation with the prophets of Baal. On Mount Carmel, he prayed, "Answer me, O Lord, answer me, so that this people will know that you, O Lord, are God" (1 Kings 18:37, ESV). Elijah's prayer was brief yet powerful, resulting in a consuming fire that confirmed God's sovereignty and silenced the false prophets. James later reflects on Elijah's prayer, emphasizing that "The prayer of a righteous person has great power as it is working" (James 5:16, ESV). Elijah's example underscores that prayer is not about eloquence but faith and alignment with God's purposes.

In the New Testament, Jesus' prayer life provides the ultimate model for believers. He withdrew to solitary places to pray (Mark 1:35), spending hours in communion with the Father before major decisions and events. His prayer life was marked by consistency, intimacy, and submission. In Gethsemane, Jesus prayed with such intensity that "his sweat became like great drops of blood falling to the ground" (Luke 22:44, ESV). This prayer was a profound act of surrender, aligning Jesus' will with the Father's and preparing Him to endure the cross. Gethsemane reveals that true prayer is not about escaping suffering but embracing God's will amidst suffering.

Furthermore, Jesus taught His disciples to pray with both faith and persistence. In Luke 18:1–8, He tells the parable of the persistent widow, encouraging believers to "always pray and not lose heart." This parable reveals that God values persistence in prayer, not because He is reluctant to answer but because prayer deepens faith, aligns desires, and cultivates spiritual endurance. Jesus concludes the parable with a rhetorical question: "When the Son of Man comes, will he find faith on the earth?" (Luke 18:8, ESV). This statement suggests that faith and prayer are inseparably linked—persistent prayer is a manifestation of enduring faith.

The apostles also modeled the power of prayer in the early church. After Jesus' ascension, the disciples "devoted themselves to prayer" (Acts 1:14), seeking guidance, empowerment, and unity. In Acts 4, Peter and John prayed for boldness after being threatened by religious leaders. Their prayer resulted in a physical manifestation of God's power: "And when they had prayed, the place in which they were gathered together was shaken" (Acts 4:31, ESV). This event underscores that prayer is not merely a private act of devotion but a corporate act that can provoke divine intervention and empower the church to fulfill its mission.

Paul, too, consistently emphasized the power of prayer in his epistles. In Ephesians 6:18, he instructs believers to "pray at all times in the Spirit, with all prayer and supplication." For Paul, prayer was not an occasional exercise but a continual engagement with God's presence, a spiritual weapon to be wielded in every circumstance. He prayed fervently for the churches he planted, asking God to fill them with wisdom, revelation, and spiritual strength (Eph. 1:16–17; Col. 1:9–11).

Thus, prayer is portrayed throughout Scripture as a dynamic, powerful practice that invites divine intervention, aligns human will with divine purpose, and manifests God's power in tangible ways. It is a spiritual discipline that not only changes circumstances but also transforms the heart, building faith, deepening trust, and revealing the character of God to those who pray.

Jesus' prayer life provides the ultimate model. He withdrew to solitary places to pray (Mark 1:35), spending hours in communion with the Father before major decisions and events. In Gethsemane, Jesus prayed with such intensity that "his sweat became like great drops of blood falling to the ground" (Luke

22:44, ESV). His prayer was a submission to the Father's will, a surrender that empowered Him to endure the cross.

Historical Perspectives on Prayer

Prayer has been central to the spiritual practices of believers throughout church history, shaping the lives of saints, martyrs, and reformers alike. From the early church to the modern era, prayer has been a powerful tool for spiritual formation, divine intervention, and communal unity. Each era offers unique insights into the transformative power of prayer, revealing how this practice has been both a personal discipline and a corporate mandate.

In the early church, prayer was foundational to the life of the Christian community. The apostles devoted themselves to "the prayers" as a daily discipline (Acts 2:42). Church fathers like Augustine and Athanasius emphasized prayer as a direct line of communication with God. In his Confessions, Augustine regarded prayer as the means of aligning the soul with God's will, a sacred conversation that drew the believer closer to divine reality.[30] (Augustine [397] 1998). Athanasius taught that prayer was a defense against spiritual darkness and a way to access God's power in times of trial.

The monastic tradition further developed prayer as a central spiritual practice. Desert Fathers like Anthony the Great retreated into solitude to cultivate a life of ceaseless prayer, seeking uninterrupted communion with God. Benedict of Nursia formalized this practice through the *Rule of St. Benedict*, which structured daily life around set hours of prayer and Scripture

---

[30] Augustine. [397] 1998. *Confessions*. Translated by Henry Chadwick. Oxford: Oxford University Press.

reading. For Benedictines, prayer was a daily ritual and a continuous state of being—*ora et labora* (pray and work).

During the Reformation, Martin Luther and John Calvin emphasized the necessity of fervent, faith-filled prayer. Luther famously declared, "To be a Christian without prayer is no more possible than to be alive without breathing."[31] He advocated prayer as a personal and communal act, aligning with God's will and seeking divine strength in times of persecution and hardship.

John Calvin echoed this sentiment, asserting that prayer is "the chief exercise of faith by which we daily receive God's benefits."[32] For Calvin, prayer was not a mechanical ritual but a vital expression of faith and dependence on God's sovereignty. He believed that through prayer, believers actively participated in God's providential work, bringing their needs, praises, and petitions before the throne of grace.

In the 18th century, the Methodist revival led by John Wesley placed a renewed emphasis on prayer as a communal and transformative practice. Wesley's "Holy Club" engaged in regular, scheduled times of prayer, confession, and intercession, fostering accountability and spiritual growth. Wesley believed prayer was essential to sanctification, a means of drawing nearer to God and conforming to the image of Christ.

The 20th century witnessed powerful movements of prayer that shaped global history. Intercessors like Rees Howells demonstrated the power of prevailing prayer during World War

---

[31] Luther, Martin. 1966. *Luther's Works, Vol. 35: Word and Sacrament I.* Edited by E. Theodore Bachmann. Philadelphia: Fortress Press.
[32] Calvin, John. [1559] 2008. *Institutes of the Christian Religion.* Translated by Henry Beveridge. Peabody, MA: Hendrickson Publishers

II. Howells and his prayer group at the Bible College of Wales engaged in prolonged intercession for specific battles and geopolitical events, aligning their petitions with the guidance of the Holy Spirit. His life exemplifies how prayer can shape history when surrendered to God's will.

Modern voices like Dietrich Bonhoeffer and Dallas Willard have continued to emphasize the centrality of prayer. In Life Together, Bonhoeffer taught that prayer is a discipline that cultivates spiritual maturity and fosters unity within the body of Christ.[33] In The Spirit of the Disciplines, Willard warned against the superficial engagement with prayer, urging believers to practice sustained, focused prayer that leads to inner transformation.[34]

Thus, the historical emphasis on prayer reveals a consistent theme: spiritual giants across centuries did not merely recite prayers—they lived them, embodying the practice as a way of life. Their legacies call modern believers to reclaim prayer as a powerful, life-altering practice—a means of encountering God, interceding for others, and participating in unfolding His redemptive plan.

In the modern era, intercessors like Rees Howells demonstrated the power of prevailing prayer. During World War II, Howells and his prayer group prayed for specific outcomes in battles, aligning their petitions with the guidance of the Holy

---

[33] Bonhoeffer, Dietrich. 1954. *Life Together*. Translated by John W. Doberstein. New York: Harper & Row.
[34] Willard, Dallas. 1998. *The Spirit of the Disciplines: Understanding How God Changes Lives*. San Francisco: Harper, San Francisco

Spirit. His life exemplifies how prayer can shape history when surrendered to the will of God.

Practical Habits for a Consistent Prayer Life

1. **Establish a Sacred Time and Space:** Designate a specific time and place for prayer each day. This consistency creates a rhythm of expectation, fostering a more profound connection with God.

2. **Pray the Scriptures:** Integrate passages from the Psalms, the Lord's Prayer, and Pauline prayers into your prayer life. These prayers provide language for praise and petition, grounding prayer in biblical truth.

3. **Journaling as Prayer:** Record prayers, reflections, and responses to God's voice. This practice documents spiritual growth and serves as a tangible reminder of God's faithfulness over time.

4. **Silent Prayer and Listening:** Cultivate moments of silence in prayer, allowing space to listen for the Spirit's prompting. Prayer is not merely about speaking but also about being still and knowing He is God (Ps. 46:10).

5. **Intercession:** Pray intentionally for others, standing in the gap as Moses did. Keep a list of prayer requests, revisiting them regularly to witness how God responds.

6. **Prayer Walks:** Walk and pray, using the surroundings as prompts to intercede for the community, family, and world. This practice integrates movement and prayer, making every step an act of intercession.

Obstacles to Effective Prayer

Despite its power, prayer can often feel difficult or ineffective. Common obstacles include distraction, doubt, discouragement, and spiritual warfare. These barriers can hinder the believer's ability to maintain a consistent and impactful prayer life, and overcoming them requires intentional strategies rooted in Scripture and spiritual discipline.

1. **Distraction:** In a world of constant noise, creating space for uninterrupted prayer requires intentionality and discipline. The digital age bombards believers with notifications, social media, and an endless stream of information, pulling attention away from focused prayer. Jesus withdrew to desolate places to pray, modeling the importance of removing distractions to focus on communion with the Father (Luke 5:16). Practicing silence and solitude can counteract the noise, creating a sacred space for deep, undistracted prayer.

2. **Doubt:** Doubt can undermine the effectiveness of prayer, causing believers to question whether God hears or responds. James writes, "But let him ask in faith, with no doubting, for the one who doubts is like a wave of the sea that is driven and tossed by the wind" (James 1:6, ESV). Faith is the key to accessing the power of prayer, yet faith must be rooted in the knowledge of God's character and promises. To overcome doubt, believers must anchor their prayers in Scripture, reminding themselves of God's faithfulness and sovereignty (1 John 5:14–15).

3. **Discouragement:** Discouragement often arises when prayers seem unanswered or when the desired outcome is

delayed. The parable of the persistent widow in Luke 18:1–8 illustrates the importance of perseverance in prayer. Jesus encourages believers to "always pray and not lose heart" (Luke 18:1, ESV). Perseverance is not about wearing God down but aligning our hearts with His purposes, trusting His timing is perfect. Journaling prayers and recording God's responses can be a powerful reminder of His ongoing work and faithfulness.

4. **Spiritual Warfare:** Prayer is a battleground where spiritual opposition is often encountered. Paul warns, "For we do not wrestle against flesh and blood, but against the rulers, against the authorities, against the cosmic powers over this present darkness" (Eph. 6:12, ESV). The enemy seeks to distract, discourage, and dissuade believers from praying effectively. Spiritual warfare requires vigilance and discernment, utilizing the whole armor of God, especially the "sword of the Spirit, which is the word of God," and "praying at all times in the Spirit" (Eph. 6:17–18, ESV).

5. **Unconfessed Sin:** Sin can act as a barrier between the believer and God, hindering the effectiveness of prayer. David acknowledged this reality, stating, "If I had cherished iniquity in my heart, the Lord would not have listened" (Ps. 66:18, ESV). Confession and repentance restore the line of communication, removing the spiritual blockage and reestablishing intimacy with God. As 1 John 1:9 affirms, "If we confess our sins, he is faithful and just to forgive us our sins and to cleanse us from all unrighteousness."

6. **Lack of Focus:** Prayer requires a deliberate focus on God's presence, yet many believers struggle with wandering thoughts and mental distractions. To combat this, structured prayer—such as the ACTS model (Adoration, Confession, Thanksgiving, Supplication)— can provide a framework for maintaining focus and intentionality. Additionally, praying through Scripture allows believers to align their words with God's Word, transforming prayer into a dialogue with the Divine.

7. **Impatience:** In a culture of instant gratification, waiting on God can feel counterintuitive. However, Scripture repeatedly emphasizes the importance of patience in prayer. The psalmist declares, "Wait for the Lord; be strong, and let your heart take courage; wait for the Lord!" (Ps. 27:14, ESV). Waiting is not passive but active faith, trusting that God is working behind the scenes, even when immediate answers are not evident.

Addressing these obstacles requires more than willpower— it requires a strategic, Spirit-led approach. By cultivating a habit of structured, Scripture-based prayer, maintaining spiritual vigilance, and persevering in faith, believers can overcome these barriers and experience the transformative power of consistent, effectual prayer.

Conclusion: The Transformative Power of Prayer

Prayer is not a last resort but the believer's first line of defense and source of strength. The spiritual discipline connects the finite with the Infinite, the natural with the supernatural. In prayer, the believer speaks to God and listens, aligning the heart with the divine will. Jesus, our ultimate model, demonstrated that prayer was the source of His strength, the secret to His ministry, and the sustenance of His soul.

When prayer becomes a way of life, it becomes the conduit through which God's power flows, transforming situations, shaping destinies, and molding hearts. The believer who strengthens the line of prayer becomes a vessel through which God's will is accomplished on earth as in heaven. Thus, prayer is a call to deeper intimacy, greater faith, and unshakable trust in the One who hears and answers every cry.

Chapter 4

Live Grateful, Worship Fully — Cultivating a Heart of Praise and Thankfulness

Gratitude and worship are foundational elements of the Christian life, serving as spiritual disciplines that align the believer's heart with the nature and character of God. In a world consumed by materialism, self-focus, and discontentment, the call to live gratefully and worship fully stands as a radical, countercultural act of faith. This chapter explores the theological significance of thankfulness, the biblical call to worship, and the transformative impact of cultivating a heart of praise. By examining scriptural teachings, historical perspectives, and practical applications, we will uncover how living in a state of perpetual gratitude and worship reshapes our perspective, strengthens our faith, and deepens our connection to God.

The Theology of Gratitude and Worship

Theologically, gratitude is far more than a mere expression of thanks; it is a profound recognition of God's sovereignty, goodness, and faithfulness. Paul declares, "Give thanks in all circumstances; for this is the will of God in Christ Jesus for you" (1 Thess. 5:18, ESV). This exhortation reveals that thanksgiving is not contingent upon favorable circumstances but is a posture of the heart that acknowledges God's unwavering presence in every situation. Gratitude, therefore, becomes a declaration of trust in God's providence, affirming that He is both sovereign and good even amidst trials and uncertainties.

Gratitude is deeply rooted in the recognition that every good and perfect gift comes from God (James 1:17). It is a response to His grace, a declaration that all we have and all we are is a result of His benevolence. By practicing gratitude, believers align themselves with the truth that God is the ultimate source of provision, protection, and purpose. This theological foundation anchors gratitude not in temporal blessings but in the eternal character of God, making it an act of worship regardless of circumstance.

Worship, on the other hand, is the outward expression of inward gratitude. It is ascribing worth to God, acknowledging His holiness, majesty, and authority. Worship is not confined to singing songs or attending services; it is a lifestyle of adoration and reverence that encompasses every aspect of the believer's life. Jesus emphasized this in John 4:24, declaring, "God is spirit, and those who worship him must worship in spirit and truth." This form of worship transcends ritual and tradition, focusing instead on the heart posture that responds to God's revealed nature with awe and reverence.

Moreover, the union of gratitude and worship is profoundly expressed in the Psalms, where thanksgiving and praise are often interwoven. The psalmist proclaims, "I will give thanks to the Lord with my whole heart; I will recount all of your wonderful deeds" (Ps. 9:1, ESV). Here, gratitude leads naturally to worship, and worship serves as a reminder of God's past faithfulness, reinforcing the believer's trust in His continued provision.

Calvin articulates this connection well, asserting that "gratitude and worship are the chief exercises of faith by which we daily receive God's benefits."[35] For Calvin, the believer's recognition of God's goodness should naturally overflow into expressions of praise and adoration, thus completing the cycle of receiving and responding.

In the New Testament, Paul consistently links gratitude and worship as essential components of the believer's spiritual life. In Colossians 3:16–17, he instructs, "Let the word of Christ dwell in you richly... singing psalms and hymns and spiritual songs, with thankfulness in your hearts to God." Here, the indwelling Word produces a heart of thanksgiving that finds expression in songs of worship, illustrating that true worship is rooted in gratitude for the revelation of Christ.

Thus, gratitude and worship are inseparable in the life of the believer. Gratitude shifts the heart from entitlement to humility, acknowledging that every blessing is a gift of grace. Worship, in turn, shifts the mind from self to God, centering the believer's focus on His unchanging nature. Together, they form a powerful spiritual dynamic that transforms perspective, deepens faith, and fosters a life marked by continual praise and thanksgiving.

Biblical Foundations of Thankfulness

The call to live gratefully is intricately woven throughout Scripture, beginning in the Old Testament and continuing through the New Testament. Gratitude is not merely a suggestion; it is a divine mandate that aligns the believer's heart

---

[35] Calvin, John. [1559] 2008. *Institutes of the Christian Religion*. Translated by Henry Beveridge. Peabody, MA: Hendrickson Publishers

with the character of God. The psalmist declares, "Enter his gates with thanksgiving, and his courts with praise! Give thanks to him; bless his name!" (Ps. 100:4, ESV). This invitation to approach God with a heart of gratitude underscores the connection between thanksgiving and worship, indicating that a grateful heart is a gateway to God's presence.

In the Old Testament, gratitude was often expressed through sacrifices and offerings. Leviticus 7:12 describes the "thanksgiving offering," a voluntary act of worship in response to God's provision and faithfulness. This act of giving was a tangible expression of gratitude and a communal declaration of God's goodness. The Israelites were commanded to give thanks not only for personal blessings but for the corporate deliverance and protection of the nation (Deut. 8:10-11).

Gratitude is further illustrated in the lives of key biblical figures. David, known as a man after God's own heart, exemplified a life of thanksgiving through his psalms of praise. In Psalm 103, he declares, "Bless the Lord, O my soul, and forget not all his benefits" (Ps. 103:2, ESV). David's gratitude is not limited to moments of victory; he continues to praise God even in times of distress, revealing that thankfulness is rooted not in circumstances but in God's unchanging nature.

In the New Testament, Jesus models a life of continual thanksgiving. Before performing the miracle of feeding the 5,000, He "took the loaves, and when he had given thanks, he distributed them" (John 6:11, ESV). Jesus' act of giving thanks before the miracle signifies that gratitude precedes divine provision. Similarly, at the Last Supper, Jesus gave thanks before breaking the bread, knowing that it symbolized His impending suffering and sacrifice (Luke 22:19). His thanksgiving in the face of suffering underscores that gratitude is not contingent upon favorable outcomes but is an acknowledgment of God's sovereignty and purpose.

Paul continues this theme in his epistles, emphasizing the centrality of gratitude in the believer's life. In Ephesians 5:20, he instructs, "Give thanks always and for everything to God the Father in the name of our Lord Jesus Christ." For Paul, thanksgiving was not a circumstantial response but a continual attitude that permeates every aspect of the believer's existence. He reinforces this in Philippians 4:6, urging believers to "not be anxious about anything, but in everything by prayer and supplication with thanksgiving let your requests be made known to God." Here, gratitude is positioned as a countermeasure to anxiety, a spiritual discipline that fosters trust in God's faithfulness.

Thus, the biblical foundation of gratitude is not passive acknowledgment but active remembrance of God's goodness, faithfulness, and provision. It is a deliberate choice to focus on what God has done, regardless of present circumstances, cultivating a heart anchored in praise and thanksgiving.

Historical Perspectives on Praise and Worship

Throughout church history, praise and worship have been more than ritualistic practices—they have been vital spiritual disciplines that shaped the faith, sustained the soul, and strengthened the community of believers. The roots of praise and worship are evident in the early church, where believers gathered to sing hymns, recite psalms, and offer prayers of thanksgiving. Acts 2:42 records that the early Christians "devoted themselves to the apostles' teaching and the fellowship, to the breaking of bread and the prayers." Worship was not merely a Sunday event but a daily expression of communal faith and unity.

The early church fathers, such as Augustine and Athanasius, emphasized the transformative power of praise and worship. Augustine viewed worship as a means of reorienting the heart from earthly desires to divine realities. In his *Confessions*, he declared, "You have made us for yourself, O Lord, and our heart is restless until it rests in you"[36] (Augustine [397] 1998). For Augustine, worship was a recognition of God's sovereignty and a declaration of the soul's dependence upon Him.

Athanasius, known for his defense of orthodox Christianity against Arianism, emphasized the centrality of the Psalms in worship. He taught that the Psalms were a divine gift, a means by which believers could articulate every emotion—joy, sorrow, repentance, and praise. Athanasius instructed the faithful to pray the Psalms daily, asserting that they encapsulate the entirety of the human experience in dialogue with God.

In the monastic tradition, praise and worship became structured practices of daily devotion. The Rule of St. Benedict established a rigorous schedule of prayer, known as the *Divine Office*, which included chanting psalms, hymns, and prayers at set hours throughout the day. This discipline of continual praise and worship fostered a rhythm of spiritual awareness, reminding the monks that God's presence permeates every moment of life.

During the Reformation, Martin Luther restored congregational singing to corporate worship, emphasizing that praise was not only the responsibility of the clergy but the

---

[36] Augustine. [397] 1998. *Confessions*. Translated by Henry Chadwick. Oxford: Oxford University Press.

privilege of every believer. He composed hymns rich in theological content, declaring that music was a divine gift that could lift the soul heavenward. Luther proclaimed, "Next to the Word of God, the noble art of music is the greatest treasure in the world."[37] Worship through song became a means of uniting the church, proclaiming doctrine, and expressing heartfelt gratitude.

John Calvin also emphasized the significance of corporate worship. In Geneva, he introduced the practice of singing metrical psalms, believing that the words of Scripture set to music could instruct, edify, and inspire the congregation. For Calvin, worship was a sacred dialogue between God and His people, a moment when heaven and earth intersect through prayer, song, and the proclamation of the Word.[38]

In modern times, worship has evolved from structured liturgies to more spontaneous and expressive forms. Leaders such as Dietrich Bonhoeffer emphasized that worship is a vertical expression of praise to God and a horizontal act of unity among believers. In *Life Together*, he writes, "It is in worship that the congregation becomes the Body of Christ, united in one spirit, one faith, and one voice"[39]

Dallas Willard, a contemporary voice in spiritual formation, emphasized the role of worship as a means of centering the heart and mind on God's presence. He taught that worship is not limited to a church service but encompasses all

---

[37] Luther, Martin. 1966. *Luther's Works, Vol. 35: Word and Sacrament I.* Edited by E. Theodore Bachmann. Philadelphia: Fortress Press
[38] Calvin, John. [1559] 2008. *Institutes of the Christian Religion.* Translated by Henry Beveridge. Peabody, MA: Hendrickson Publishers
[39] Bonhoeffer, Dietrich. 1954. *Life Together.* Translated by John W. Doberstein. New York: Harper & Row

life. In *The Spirit of the Disciplines*, he writes, "Worship is the single most powerful force in completing and sustaining restoration in the whole person"[40]

Thus, the historical perspectives on praise and worship reveal a rich tradition of believers who recognized the transformative power of praise. Whether through psalms, hymns, chants, or contemporary worship songs, worship has always been a profound declaration of God's worthiness and the believer's gratitude. This legacy calls modern believers to reclaim worship as a way of life, a continual act of reverence and praise that transcends circumstance and elevates the soul into the presence of God.

Practical Habits for Cultivating Gratitude and Worship

1. **Daily Thanksgiving Journal:** Begin each day by writing down three things you are grateful for. This practice shifts the focus from lack to abundance, training the mind to recognize God's blessings.

2. **Worship Walks:** Take a walk and intentionally praise God for the beauty of creation, expressing gratitude for the natural world and God's sustaining power.

3. **Scripture-Focused Worship:** Select a psalm or hymn and pray through it, allowing its words to guide your praise and direct your focus to God's attributes.

---

[40] Willard, Dallas. 1998. *The Spirit of the Disciplines: Understanding How God Changes Lives.* San Francisco: HarperSanFrancisco

4. **Intentional Acts of Kindness:** Show gratitude through service. Bless someone with a gift, note, or act of kindness, extending God's love and goodness to others.

5. **Prayer of Examen:** At the end of each day, reflect on where you experienced God's presence and where gratitude was lacking. Ask the Holy Spirit to cultivate a heart of thanksgiving.

Obstacles to Grateful Living

Despite its transformative power, cultivating a life of gratitude and worship can be challenging, particularly in a culture that often fosters entitlement, comparison, and discontentment. Identifying and addressing these obstacles is essential for maintaining a heart centered on God's goodness and faithfulness.

1. **Comparison and Envy:** In a world driven by social media and constant comparison, believers can easily fall into the trap of measuring their blessings against those of others. The psalmist cautions against such envy, stating, "Fret not yourself because of evildoers; be not envious of wrongdoers!" (Ps. 37:1, ESV). Comparison shifts the focus from God's unique provision to what others possess, eroding a sense of gratitude and fostering discontentment. Overcoming this requires a conscious effort to focus on God's specific blessings and to cultivate a spirit of thanksgiving for what has been entrusted to us.

2. **Entitlement:** Entitlement is the antithesis of gratitude. This mindset assumes God's blessings are deserved rather than graciously given. This perspective is evident in the parable of the workers in the vineyard (Matt. 20:1–

16), where those who worked longer hours felt entitled to more pay than those who worked less. Jesus' response emphasizes that God's generosity is not based on human standards but on His sovereign will. Recognizing that every gift is an act of grace fosters humility and thankfulness, redirecting the heart from entitlement to gratitude.

3. **Discontentment:** The apostle Paul addresses the issue of discontentment in Philippians 4:11–12, stating, "I have learned in whatever situation I am to be content." Contentment is not a natural state but a learned discipline, cultivated through trust in God's provision and faithfulness. Discontentment often arises from a desire for more possessions, recognition, or success. Combatting discontentment requires a deliberate focus on God's sufficiency, embracing the truth that "godliness with contentment is great gain" (1 Tim. 6:6, ESV).

4. **Busyness and Distraction:** In a culture that celebrates productivity and busyness, finding time to pause, reflect, and give thanks can be difficult. Jesus modeled the practice of withdrawing to solitary places to pray (Luke 5:16), creating space to commune with the Father without distraction. Cultivating gratitude requires intentional slowing down, creating rhythms of reflection, and setting aside time to acknowledge God's presence and blessings.

5. **Forgetfulness:** The Israelites often fell into the trap of forgetting God's faithfulness, particularly after experiencing His miraculous provision. Moses warned them, "Take care lest you forget the Lord your God, who brought you out of the land of Egypt" (Deut. 8:11, ESV).

Forgetfulness breeds ingratitude, leading the heart to focus on current challenges rather than past deliverances. Journaling, prayer, and regular reflection on God's past faithfulness can serve as powerful antidotes to spiritual amnesia.

6. **Bitterness and Unforgiveness:** Holding onto offenses and nursing grudges can harden the heart against gratitude. Hebrews 12:15 warns, "See to it that no one fails to obtain the grace of God; that no root of bitterness springs up and causes trouble." Bitterness not only corrodes the soul but also blinds the heart to God's ongoing blessings. Releasing offenses through forgiveness opens the heart to gratitude, allowing the believer to see God's goodness even amidst pain.

7. **Fear and Anxiety:** Fear and anxiety can overshadow gratitude, causing believers to focus on what might go wrong rather than what God has already done. Paul addresses this in Philippians 4:6–7, instructing believers to "not be anxious about anything, but in everything by prayer and supplication with thanksgiving let your requests be made known to God." Gratitude serves as a stabilizing force, redirecting the mind from fear to faith, from anxiety to assurance in God's unwavering faithfulness.

Overcoming these obstacles requires intentional practice, continual reflection, and a commitment to cultivating a heart centered on God's goodness. As believers choose to practice gratitude and worship, they are empowered to break free from the chains of comparison, entitlement, and discontentment, embracing a life marked by praise, thanksgiving, and spiritual contentment.

Conclusion: Living a Life of Grateful Worship

Living a life of gratitude and worship is not about denying life's difficulties but about choosing to focus on God's unchanging goodness amidst them. When gratitude becomes a lifestyle, it transforms perspective, shifting the believer from a posture of self-centeredness to one of God-centeredness. Worship, in turn, becomes the natural overflow of a heart that acknowledges God's grace and sovereignty.

A heart of gratitude fosters resilience in trials, contentment in scarcity, and faith in uncertainty. A worship life anchors the soul in God's presence, producing spiritual stability and enduring joy. Thus, the call to live grateful and worship entirely is a call to align the heart with God's purposes, embrace His goodness, and proclaim His faithfulness in every circumstance.

Chapter 5

Renew Your Mind Daily — Transforming Your Life by Changing Your Thoughts

Transformation begins in the mind. How a believer thinks influences every aspect of their life — their actions, decisions, and spiritual growth. Paul urges, "Do not be conformed to this world, but be transformed by the renewal of your mind" (Rom. 12:2, ESV). This command reveals that transformation is not merely an emotional or behavioral change but a profound internal shift in thinking that aligns the mind with God's truth. In this chapter, we will explore the theological foundation of mind renewal, its biblical basis, the example of Jesus, and practical steps for cultivating a transformed thought life rooted in Scripture.

The Theology of Mind Renewal

Theologically, the renewal of the mind is foundational to spiritual transformation. At its core, it involves the process of aligning one's thoughts, desires, and intentions with the mind of Christ. The Greek term for 'renewal' in Romans 12:2, *anakainosis*, signifies a complete renovation — a fundamental change in how a person thinks, perceives, and interprets reality. This transformation is not superficial but penetrates the deepest recesses of the mind, reshaping thought patterns, belief systems, and perspectives to reflect divine truth.

In Pauline theology, the mind is the primary battleground where spiritual warfare occurs. Paul asserts, "For though we walk in the flesh, we do not wage war according to the flesh. The weapons of our warfare are not of the flesh but have divine power to destroy strongholds. We destroy arguments and every lofty opinion raised against the knowledge of God, and take every thought captive to obey Christ" (2 Cor. 10:3–5, ESV). Here, the mind is portrayed as the battlefield where the truth of Scripture dismantles arguments, opinions, and false ideologies.

John Calvin emphasized the mind's critical role in spiritual renewal, asserting that the human mind, in its fallen state, is a 'factory of idols' — constantly producing false beliefs, misguided ambitions, and selfish desires.[41] Therefore, mind renewal involves the deconstruction of these idols and reconstructing thought processes based on God's revealed Word. Calvin contends that until the mind is renewed, the heart remains enslaved to carnal desires, making the believer susceptible to deception and sin.

Augustine also underscored the necessity of mind renewal, particularly in his *Confessions*. He writes, "Thou hast made us for thyself, O Lord, and our heart is restless until it finds rest in thee."[42] Augustine's theological framework emphasizes that a restless, wandering mind cannot experience true peace until it is anchored in God's truth. For Augustine, mind renewal

---

[41] Calvin, John. [1559] 2008. *Institutes of the Christian Religion*. Translated by Henry Beveridge. Peabody, MA: Hendrickson Publishers
[42] Augustine. [397] 1998. *Confessions*. Translated by Henry Chadwick. Oxford: Oxford University Press

is a journey of redirecting the heart's desires from temporal pleasures to eternal realities.

Dietrich Bonhoeffer connects mind renewal to the concept of spiritual formation in *Life Together*. He argues that the mind must be disciplined through consistent exposure to God's Word and communal worship, stating, "The mind that is set on the flesh is hostile to God; it does not submit to God's law; indeed, it cannot" (Rom. 8:7, ESV). Bonhoeffer asserts that "the undisciplined mind is easily swayed by worldly influences, but the renewed mind, saturated with Scripture, discerns truth from falsehood and remains steadfast in faith."[43]

Dallas Willard expands on this in *The Spirit of the Disciplines*, identifying the mind as the gateway to spiritual transformation. He writes, "What occupies our mind ultimately shapes our life. Therefore, the renewal of the mind is the key to spiritual growth and transformation."[44] Willard emphasizes that the renewal process involves continually reorienting the mind from worldly patterns to kingdom principles, allowing the believer to perceive reality through the lens of God's Word.

Thus, theologically, the renewal of the mind is not merely an intellectual exercise but a comprehensive transformation that engages the mind, heart, and will. It is a sanctifying process facilitated by the Holy Spirit, through which the believer learns to think God's thoughts, reject false ideologies, and embrace divine truth as the ultimate standard for living.

---

[43] Bonhoeffer, Dietrich. 1954. *Life Together*. Translated by John W. Doberstein. New York: Harper & Row
[44] Willard, Dallas. 1998. *The Spirit of the Disciplines: Understanding How God Changes Lives*. San Francisco: HarperSanFrancisco

Biblical Foundations of Thought Transformation

Scripture consistently emphasizes the importance of correct thinking as a precursor to right living. The biblical mandate to renew the mind is rooted in recognizing that thoughts shape actions, and actions shape destiny. Proverbs 23:7 declares, "For as he thinks in his heart, so is he" (NKJV), underscoring that a person's internal thought life profoundly influences their external reality. In the Hebrew mindset, the heart and mind were not separate; they were viewed as the seat of intentions, desires, and will. Thus, transforming one's life necessitates first transforming one's thoughts.

Paul's exhortation to the Philippians provides a practical framework for thought transformation: "Finally, brothers, whatever is true, whatever is honorable, whatever is just, whatever is pure, whatever is lovely, whatever is commendable, if there is any excellence, if there is anything worthy of praise, think about these things" (Phil. 4:8, ESV). This directive is not merely a call to positive thinking but a profound invitation to intentionally focus on thoughts that reflect the character of God. Each attribute listed by Paul corresponds to aspects of God's nature, urging believers to adopt a heavenly perspective in their daily thought life.

Romans 12:2 serves as the cornerstone text for mind renewal: "Do not be conformed to this world, but be transformed by the renewal of your mind." The Greek term for "transformed," *metamorphoo*, denotes a complete metamorphosis, similar to the radical change from a caterpillar to a butterfly. This transformation is not cosmetic; it is a fundamental shift in how the believer perceives reality, moving from a worldly mindset to a kingdom perspective. Paul asserts that the renewed mind enables the believer to discern "what is the good and acceptable and perfect will of God," suggesting that correct thinking is essential for spiritual discernment.

In 2 Corinthians 10:5, Paul further elaborates on mental transformation: "We destroy arguments and every lofty opinion raised against the knowledge of God, and take every thought captive to obey Christ." Here, the mind is depicted as a battlefield where destructive thoughts, lies, and false ideologies must be confronted and brought into submission to the truth of God's Word. Taking thoughts captive is not passive; it is an active, Spirit-led discipline that requires vigilance, discernment, and intentionality.

The connection between thoughts and spiritual warfare is evident in Ephesians 6:17, where Paul describes the "helmet of salvation" as part of the believer's armor. The helmet protects the mind, symbolizing the necessity of safeguarding one's thoughts against enemy attacks. The helmet is paired with the "sword of the Spirit, which is the Word of God," indicating that the mind is defended and renewed by the truth of Scripture.

Jesus also addressed the importance of correct thinking in the Sermon on the Mount, urging His followers to avoid anxious, fearful thoughts that undermine faith: "Therefore do not be anxious, saying, 'What shall we eat?' or 'What shall we drink?' or 'What shall we wear?'... But seek first the kingdom of God and his righteousness" (Matt. 6:31–33, ESV). Jesus' teaching underscores that anxious thoughts are often rooted in misplaced focus and a lack of trust in God's provision. Renewing the mind involves redirecting such thoughts toward the sovereignty and faithfulness of God.

Thus, the biblical foundation for thought transformation is firmly established throughout Scripture. From the Proverbs to the Pauline epistles, the consistent message is clear: thoughts are powerful, shaping identity, influencing behavior, and ultimately determining destiny. The believer's call to renew the mind is not a one-time event but a continuous, Spirit-led process of aligning every thought with the truth of God's Word.

In Romans 8:5–6, Paul contrasts the mind set on the flesh with the mind set on the Spirit: "For those who live according to the flesh set their minds on the things of the flesh, but those who live according to the Spirit set their minds on the things of the Spirit." A mind set on the flesh leads to spiritual death, but a mind set on the Spirit leads to life and peace. Thus, thought transformation is not a passive process but an active, Spirit-led endeavor that requires continual vigilance and intentionality.

The Mind of Christ: Jesus as the Model for Renewed Thinking

Jesus is the ultimate model of a mind fully surrendered to God's will. Throughout His earthly ministry, Jesus consistently demonstrated a mind anchored in the truth of Scripture and aligned with the Father's purposes. The Gospels present multiple instances where Jesus exemplified the principles of a renewed mind, resisting temptation, rejecting worldly influences, and embracing the divine will even in the face of suffering.

In the wilderness, Satan tried to entice Jesus to act independently of God's provision and purpose. Jesus responded to each temptation with Scripture, declaring, "It is written," three times, each time countering Satan's lies with the truth of God's Word (Matt. 4:1–11). This encounter illustrates that the renewed mind is not one that merely acknowledges Scripture but wields it as a sword against deception. By wielding the Word as His primary weapon, Jesus demonstrated that a mind saturated in Scripture is resistant to deception and fortified against the enemy's attacks.

Paul urges believers to "have this mind among yourselves, which is yours in Christ Jesus" (Phil. 2:5, ESV). This call to adopt the mind of Christ involves embracing humility, selflessness, and obedience to the Father. Paul continues, "Though he was in the form of God, did not count equality with God a thing to be grasped, but emptied himself, taking the form of a servant" (Phil. 2:6–7, ESV). Jesus' willingness to empty Himself of divine privilege and submit to the Father's will exemplifies a renewed mind that is not driven by self-interest but by divine purpose.

In Gethsemane, Jesus further exemplifies a mind wholly surrendered to God's will. Facing imminent suffering, He prays, "Not my will, but yours be done" (Luke 22:42, ESV). This prayer encapsulates the essence of a renewed mind—a mind that prioritizes God's will over personal comfort and seeks divine purposes even amid pain. Jesus' submission in Gethsemane reveals that the renewed mind is not immune to suffering but is empowered to endure suffering with grace and faith.

Moreover, Jesus demonstrated the principle of mind renewal through His teachings on anxiety and worry. In the Sermon on the Mount, He instructs His followers, "Therefore do not be anxious, saying, 'What shall we eat?' or 'What shall we drink?' or 'What shall we wear?'... But seek first the kingdom of

God and his righteousness" (Matt. 6:31–33, ESV). Jesus emphasized that a mind focused on God's kingdom is free from anxiety, rooted in trust, and anchored in the faithfulness of God.

Paul reiterates this principle, urging believers to adopt a heavenly mindset: "Set your minds on things that are above, not on things that are on earth" (Col. 3:2, ESV). Jesus exemplified this throughout His life, consistently directing His thoughts toward heavenly realities rather than temporal concerns. Even in His final moments on the cross, Jesus prayed, "Father, forgive them, for they know not what they do" (Luke 23:34, ESV). This prayer reveals a mind that transcends personal suffering to align with the Father's redemptive mission, demonstrating that the renewed mind is not bound by earthly circumstances but is fixed on God's eternal purposes.

Thus, Jesus' life and teachings provide the quintessential model for renewing the mind. He exemplified a life of total surrender, unwavering faith, and divine focus, setting a standard for believers to emulate. By adopting the mind of Christ, believers learn to think God's thoughts, reject carnal influences, and align every thought with the truth of Scripture.

Historical Perspectives on Mind Renewal

Throughout church history, spiritual leaders have consistently emphasized the importance of mind renewal as a crucial element in the believer's spiritual growth and transformation. The early Church Fathers, Reformers, and modern theologians have each provided profound insights into the process of renewing the mind and its significance in the life of a Christian.

Augustine of Hippo was one of the earliest voices to articulate the connection between mind renewal and spiritual transformation. In his *Confessions*, he describes his own struggle with disordered thoughts and desires, ultimately finding rest in God's truth: "Thou hast made us for thyself, O Lord, and our heart is restless until it finds rest in thee"[45] For Augustine, the renewal of the mind involved redirecting one's thoughts from earthly passions to heavenly realities, recognizing that true peace and fulfillment can only be found in God.

Martin Luther viewed the mind as a battlefield, where spiritual warfare is waged against the forces of darkness. He famously stated, "The devil throws hideous thoughts into the soul — hatred of God, blasphemy, and despair."[46] Luther emphasized that the believer must actively reject these fiery darts and replace them with the truth of Scripture. For Luther, the renewed mind engaged in continual repentance and constant meditation on God's Word, allowing divine truth to dismantle the enemy's lies.

John Calvin further developed this concept, asserting that the mind is the source from which all actions flow. In the Institutes of the Christian Religion, he writes, "The human heart is an idol factory," emphasizing that the unrenewed mind is susceptible to false ideologies and sinful desires.[47] Calvin's solution was to cultivate a disciplined mind that is daily saturated with the Word of God, aligning every thought and intention with divine truth.

---

[45] Augustine. [397] 1998. *Confessions*. Translated by Henry Chadwick. Oxford: Oxford University Press.
[46] Luther, Martin. 1966. *Luther's Works, Vol. 35: Word and Sacrament I*. Edited by E. Theodore Bachmann. Philadelphia: Fortress Press
[47] Calvin, John. [1559] 2008. *Institutes of the Christian Religion*. Translated by Henry Beveridge. Peabody, MA: Hendrickson Publishers

John Wesley, the founder of Methodism, emphasized the importance of renewing the mind as a means of sanctification. In his *Sermons on Several Occasions*, Wesley urged believers to guard their minds against worldly distractions and to meditate on God's Word day and night. He likened the mind to a garden that must be continually cultivated lest it become overrun with weeds of sinful thoughts. Wesley advocated for structured prayer, Scripture reading, and self-examination as essential practices in maintaining a renewed mind.

In Life Together, Dietrich Bonhoeffer emphasized the communal aspect of mind renewal. He argued that believers are responsible not only for their own spiritual formation but also for encouraging one another to maintain a renewed perspective. "The mind that is set on the flesh is hostile to God," Bonhoeffer wrote, referencing Romans 8:7. For Bonhoeffer, the undisciplined mind is easily swayed by worldly influences, but the renewed mind, saturated with Scripture and supported by the faith community, discerns truth from falsehood and remains steadfast in faith.

Dallas Willard, a contemporary voice in spiritual formation, underscored the transformative power of the mind in his seminal work, *The Spirit of the Disciplines*. Willard argued that the mind is the gateway to spiritual growth, stating, "What occupies our mind ultimately shapes our life."[48] He taught that mind renewal involves a continual reorientation from worldly patterns to kingdom principles, allowing the believer to perceive reality through the lens of God's Word. For Willard, spiritual disciplines

---

[48] Willard, Dallas. 1998. *The Spirit of the Disciplines: Understanding How God Changes Lives*. San Francisco: HarperSanFrancisco.

such as meditation, solitude, and Scripture memorization were essential in maintaining a mind fixed on Christ.

Thus, the historical emphasis on mind renewal reveals a consistent thread: from Augustine's reflections on restless desires to Luther's battle against mental strongholds, from Calvin's focus on spiritual discipline to Willard's call for intentional thought cultivation, the church has always recognized that spiritual transformation begins in the mind. The renewed mind is a mind that thinks God's thoughts, rejects carnal influences, and remains steadfast in truth despite external pressures.

Practical Habits for Daily Mind Renewal

1. **Scripture Memorization:** Commit key verses to memory that counter negative thought patterns and reinforce God's truth.

2. **Prayer and Meditation:** Begin each day with focused prayer, asking the Holy Spirit to reveal areas of unrenewed thinking and to transform them through the Word.

3. **Thought Journaling:** Document recurring thought patterns and compare them against Scripture. Replace lies with biblical truth.

4. **Accountability Partnerships:** Share struggles with trusted spiritual mentors who can provide biblical counsel and encouragement.

5. **Intentional Media Consumption:** Limit exposure to media that fosters negativity, fear, or sinful mindsets, and replace it with content that edifies and uplifts.

Obstacles to Renewing the Mind

1. **Negative Thought Patterns:** Long-standing thought habits that contradict God's truth.

2. **Worldly Influences:** Media, culture, and relationships that perpetuate ungodly thinking.

3. **Unconfessed Sin:** Sin that distorts perspective and hinders spiritual clarity.

4. **Fear and Anxiety:** Thoughts driven by fear rather than faith, leading to spiritual stagnation.

Conclusion: The Transformative Power of a Renewed Mind

Renewing the mind is not a one-time event but a lifelong process of sanctification. As believers intentionally align their thoughts with Scripture, they undergo a transformation that reshapes their character, deepens their faith, and empowers them to discern God's will in every situation. By embracing the mind of Christ, they become vessels of divine wisdom, living testimonies of God's transformative power in a world filled with darkness and deception.

Chapter 6

Transformed in Christ – Sanctification and the Renewal of the Believer

Conversion is only the beginning of the Christian journey. After turning to Christ in repentance and faith, believers enter a process of transformation in which they progressively conformed to Christ's character. In Christian theology, this ongoing change is often called sanctification – the gradual making holy of a person's heart and life. It is the work of God's grace by which He reshapes us from the inside out to reflect the image of His Son. The goal of salvation is not merely that we escape judgment, but that we become like Jesus in our inner being: "to be conformed to the image of his Son" (Rom. 8:29, NIV).

This means that our thoughts, desires, and virtues increasingly mirror those of Christ Himself. Spiritual transformation involves a profound change of nature – what the New Testament describes as putting off the "old self" and putting on the "new self, created to be like God in true righteousness and holiness" (Eph. 4:22–24, NIV). By the power of the Holy Spirit, the traits of Christ's character (love, purity, humility, etc.) are formed in us, while the distortions of sin are gradually healed.

At its heart, transformation is an act of God's grace. Only God can fundamentally change the human heart. Scripture teaches that we who were spiritually dead have been made alive with Christ (Eph. 2:4–5) and are being renewed by the Holy Spirit (Titus 3:5–6). Thus, the foundation of our transformation is our union with Christ: by faith we are joined to Jesus, and His life begins to flow in us through the Spirit. As Jesus said, He is the vine and we are the branches; if we abide in Him, we will bear much fruit (John 15:5). Our growth in Christlikeness is empowered by God's indwelling Spirit, who produces in us the "fruit of the Spirit" – those Christlike virtues of love, joy, peace, patience, kindness, and more (Gal. 5:22–23).

Transformation is not a human self-improvement project, but a Spirit-driven metamorphosis of the person. As the Apostle Paul explains, "we all, with unveiled face, beholding the glory of the Lord, are being transformed into the same image from one degree of glory to another," and this comes "from the Lord, who is the Spirit" (2 Cor. 3:18, ESV). The Greek term for "transformed" in this verse (*metamorphoō*) indicates a radical change of form – much like a caterpillar becoming a butterfly. By gazing on the glory of Christ and walking in step with His Spirit, believers gradually change their very character and habits to resemble Christ's own holiness.

However, spiritual transformation is also a cooperative process, involving our active participation. God does the work of sanctifying us, but He calls us to respond in obedience and faith. There is a mysterious synergy at play: the Holy Spirit is the agent of change, but we are called to "work out [our] own salvation with fear and trembling," knowing that it is God who ultimately works in us (Phil. 2:12–13).

The Apostle Paul often exhorts believers to "put to death" the deeds of the sinful nature (Col. 3:5) and "put on" the virtues of the new nature (Col. 3:12–14). We are not passive spectators in our transformation; instead, by yielding to the Spirit and practicing obedience, we actively cooperate with grace. As John Owen explains, mortification of sin "from a self-strength, carried on by ways of self-invention... is the soul and substance of all false religion." True sanctification, by contrast, is wrought by the Spirit, through faith in the cross of Christ.[49]

Unlike justification (being declared righteous before God), which is an instant gift received by faith alone, sanctification is generally gradual. It unfolds throughout a Christian's life as we learn to walk in the way of Christ. Day by day, God is at work in us "to will and to work for his good pleasure" (Phil. 2:13), shaping our character through every circumstance and act of obedience. Over time, the goal is that there would be a family resemblance between Christ and His followers – that we truly become "little Christs," reflecting His love and holiness in the world.

Biblical Foundations for Transformation and Holiness

The call to Christlike transformation is firmly rooted in Scripture. The Bible teaches that God's eternal purpose for His people is that we become like His Son. Romans 8:29 declares, "For those whom [God] foreknew he also predestined to be conformed to the image of his Son, in order that [Christ] might be the firstborn among many brothers." Here we see that from eternity God planned not only to save individuals from sin, but

---

[49] John Owen, *Overcoming Sin and Temptation*, ed. Kelly M. Kapic and Justin Taylor (Wheaton, IL: Crossway, 2006), 50

to shape a family of believers to resemble Jesus, the true firstborn Son. This *imago Christi* (image of Christ) is the pattern for our lives. In salvation, God is restoring what was lost at the Fall, when humanity (made in God's image) was corrupted by sin. Christ, "the image of the invisible God" (Col. 1:15), comes to renew our divine image. Thus, the New Testament often speaks of believers being renewed in knowledge after the image of our Creator (Col. 3:10) and growing into the likeness of Christ.

Several key passages illuminate this transformative work. One foundational text is 2 Corinthians 3:18, which was mentioned above. It portrays believers as beholding the glory of the Lord (as if gazing into a mirror) and as a result "being transformed into the same image from one degree of glory to another." The context contrasts the Old Covenant, which brought condemnation, with the New Covenant in the Spirit, which brings righteousness and life. In Christ, the veil is removed from our eyes, and we can steadily contemplate the Lord's glory – primarily through Scripture and prayer. As we do so, the Spirit changes us incrementally into the image of Christ's glory. This tells us that regular exposure to the glory and goodness of Jesus is key to our transformation. Little by little, what we behold, we become. If we focus on Christ – His character, teachings, and example – the Spirit imprints that likeness upon us over time.

Another important text is Galatians 5:22–23, which lists the fruit of the Spirit. Paul contrasts the works of the flesh (the natural, sinful behaviors) with the fruit that the Holy Spirit produces in a yielded believer. "The fruit of the Spirit is love, joy, peace, patience, kindness, goodness, faithfulness, gentleness, self-control" (Gal. 5:22–23, ESV). Notably, these qualities describe the character of Jesus Himself. Christ embodied divine love, exhibited unshakeable joy and peace, showed perfect patience and kindness, and demonstrated goodness, faithfulness, gentleness, and self-mastery. The Spirit's work is essentially to reproduce the character of Christ in us, so that these virtues become the habitual pattern of our life. The term "fruit" suggests a natural outgrowth – as we remain connected to Christ (the vine), the Spirit organically grows Christlike virtues in us, much as grapes naturally grow on a healthy branch (John 15:4–5). This process requires time and cultivation; fruit does not ripen overnight. However, as we "keep in step with the Spirit" (Gal. 5:25), deliberately yielding to His guidance, our lives will increasingly show evidence of this holy fruit. In fact, the presence of these virtues is one of the primary biblical evidences that true transformation is taking place. Jesus taught that "every good tree bears good fruit" (Matt. 7:17) – meaning a life touched by God's grace will eventually bear the good fruit of righteousness.

The New Testament also provides direct commands to pursue holiness and Christlikeness, reinforcing that this is God's will for every believer. For instance, 1 Peter 1:15–16 echoes the Old Testament law by urging, "as He who called you is holy, you also be holy in all your conduct, since it is written, 'You shall be holy, for I am holy.'" Here we see that the character of God (His holiness) is the model for His children. To be "holy" means to be set apart and morally pure. God wants His people to reflect His holy character by turning away from sin and walking in obedience. Likewise, Ephesians 4:22–24 instructs believers to "put off your old self, which belongs to your former manner of life…and to put on the new self, created after the likeness of God in true righteousness and holiness." This imagery of changing clothes ("put off/put on") illustrates a deliberate renunciation of our old sinful ways and a conscious adoption of new, righteous ways – essentially acting out the transformation that the Spirit is working within. Again, the "likeness of God" language points to being conformed to Christ, who perfectly images God. In practical terms, this involves replacing vices with virtues: for example, putting off falsehood and putting on truth-telling, bitterness, and forgiveness (cf. Eph. 4:25–32).

One of the most explicit biblical images of transformation is the idea of spiritual metamorphosis by renewing the mind. Romans 12:2 famously exhorts, "Do not be conformed to this world, but be transformed by the renewal of your mind, that by testing you may discern the will of God..." (ESV). The Phillips translation vividly paraphrases, "Do not let the world around you squeeze you into its own mold, but let God re-mold your minds from within." This underscores that our transformation involves a new mindset – learning to think as Christ thinks. God's truth and perspective must progressively replace our natural thought patterns, values, and perspectives (shaped by the secular culture). The Word of God is central in this renewal. As we immerse ourselves in Scripture, our minds are washed and realigned with God's ways, which leads to changed behavior. In Jesus' own prayer to the Father, He said, "Sanctify them in the truth; your word is truth" (John 17:17). The Bible, as God's truth, has a sanctifying (purifying and transforming) effect on us. Thus, regular study and meditation on Scripture are indispensable for anyone seeking Christlike character.

Lastly, the biblical vision of transformation is tied to our identity and destiny in Christ. The Apostle Paul often addresses believers as "saints" (literally "holy ones"), indicating that in

God's sight we are already set apart for Him. Therefore, he urges that our actual conduct should match our identity. For example, in 1 Corinthians 5:7, Paul says, "Christ, our Passover lamb, has been sacrificed. Let us therefore celebrate the festival, not with the old leaven... but with the unleavened bread of sincerity and truth." Because Christ's sacrifice has made us new and spotless (positionally unleavened), we are to live in sincerity and truth (practically unleavened). The indicative (what God has done, who we are) grounds the imperative (what we must do). Moreover, Scripture points forward to the completion of our transformation in eternity. One day, our Christlikeness will be perfected. First John 3:2–3 provides great hope: "We know that when [Christ] appears, we shall be like Him, because we shall see Him as He is. Moreover, everyone who thus hopes in Him purifies himself as He is pure." The certainty of future Christlikeness motivates us to pursue purity now. The process we undergo in this life will be fulfilled when we are glorified with Christ. Until then, the New Testament calls us to press on in the journey: to "grow in the grace and knowledge of our Lord" (2 Pet. 3:18), to "make every effort to supplement our faith" with Christlike qualities (2 Pet. 1:5–8), and to strive to "attain...to mature manhood, to the measure of the stature of the fullness of Christ" (Eph. 4:13). In sum, the biblical foundation is clear: God saves us in order to transform us, and He provides both the mandate and the means for us to grow into the likeness of Jesus.

Historical Perspectives on Christlike Transformation

Throughout church history, Christian leaders and theologians have consistently emphasized the importance of inner transformation and holy character. They may have used different terms – sanctification, holiness, divinization, spiritual formation – but all understood that authentic faith leads to a changed life. Here we will explore a few historical voices (beyond those mentioned in earlier chapters) that shed light on the theology and practice of Christlike transformation.

Early Church Fathers: The earliest Christian writers saw salvation as a process of healing and renewal for the soul. As noted, St. Athanasius taught that "He was made man that we might be made God," highlighting the radical elevation of human nature by grace.[50] Similarly, St. Irenaeus (2nd cent.) spoke of the Spirit gradually habituating us to divine life – fitting us for fellowship with God. Irenaeus described redeemed humanity as advancing step by step to become more accustomed to God's glory, as a wineskin acclimates to new wine.

This developmental view underscores patience in the transformation process. In the 3rd and 4th centuries, desert monastics like St. Anthony the Great withdrew into the wilderness to battle their vices and be transformed. The Desert Fathers believed that by embracing solitude, prayer, and fasting, they could, with God's help, strip away the "false self" and let the true self in Christ emerge. One desert monk taught, "If you would be perfect, flee from the world" – not because the physical world is evil, but because social conventions and distractions can hinder the soul's purification. St. Gregory of Nyssa (c. 335–394) articulated a famous doctrine of *epektasis*, or "perpetual progress." He wrote that even in heaven the righteous will continue growing in godliness, because God is infinite and there will always be more of His goodness to discover. Gregory

---

[50] Athanasius of Alexandria, *On the Incarnation*, ed. and trans. A Religious of C.S.M.V. (Crestwood, NY: St. Vladimir's Seminary Press, 1993), 54

defined the perfect Christian life as "constant growth in the good"[51] – an ongoing transformation driven by an insatiable desire for God. This hopeful view sees our spiritual life as an ever-deepening journey into God's character, rather than a static achievement.

Medieval and Reformation Insights: In the Middle Ages, there was great emphasis on imitating Christ as the path of transformation. Thomas à Kempis (1380–1471), a devout monk, authored *The Imitation of Christ*, one of the most influential Christian devotionals ever written. In it, he urges believers to study the life of Jesus and conform themselves to Him in all things: "Whoever wishes to understand fully the words of Christ must try to pattern his whole life on that of Christ."[52]

For Thomas, intellectual knowledge of doctrine was worthless without a life that looked like Christ's life – marked by humility, obedience, and love. His writing calls us beyond mere admiration of Jesus to active emulation of Jesus. This reflects a broader medieval theme that true knowledge of God is gained not by speculation but by transformation – "taste and see that the Lord is good" by living out Christ's teachings. Later, Protestant Reformers also valued sanctification, though they carefully distinguished it from justification. The Reformers wanted to avoid any suggestion that our works earn salvation; yet they insisted that saving faith results in sanctified living. Martin Luther spoke of faith as a living, busy thing that inevitably produces good works. John Calvin described regeneration as the

---

[51] Gregory of Nyssa, "The Life of Moses," in *From Glory to Glory: Texts from Gregory of Nyssa's Mystical Writings*, selected by Jean Daniélou, trans. Herbert Musurillo (New York: Charles Scribner's Sons, 1961), 105–9.
[52] Thomas à Kempis, *The Imitation of Christ*, trans. Aloysius Croft and Harold Bolton (Mineola, NY: Dover Publications, 2003), Book 1, ch. 1.

renewal of the image of God in us, a work that begins at conversion and advances throughout life. While this book has already referenced Augustine and Calvin in earlier chapters, we can look to another stream: the Holiness movement that emerged in Methodism. John Wesley (1703–1791), the founder of Methodism, placed an extraordinary emphasis on sanctification or "Christian perfection." Wesley taught that God's grace not only pardons sin but can also cleanse the heart from inward sin in this life. He defined the "perfection" he sought in very practical terms: "By perfection I mean the humble, gentle, patient love of God and our neighbor, ruling our tempers, words, and actions."[53]

Wesley did not claim sinless perfection or absolute flawlessness; rather, he meant a mature holiness characterized by pure love – loving God with all one's heart and loving one's neighbor as oneself. According to Wesley, this kind of sanctified life was possible by entire consecration and faith in God's promise to sanctify. Many in the Methodist and later Holiness traditions testified to profound experiences of the Holy Spirit purifying their desires. While not all Christian traditions articulate sanctification exactly as Wesley did, his legacy was to renew the church's focus on holiness of heart and life as the normal expectation for a Christian. He famously told believers to seek this holiness and "continually agonize for it," by which he meant fervently strive in prayer and discipline until love fully reigns within.

Across the centuries, countless other voices have echoed the call to Christlikeness. The 16th-century Spaniard St. John of

---

[53] John Wesley, *A Plain Account of Christian Perfection* (Kansas City, MO: Beacon Hill Press, 1966), 51

the Cross described the soul's transformation through the "dark night of the soul" – seasons of trial and purgation that God uses to strip away our attachments and unite us more purely to Himself. The 19th-century Russian Orthodox saint Seraphim of Sarov taught that the aim of the Christian life is the acquisition of the Holy Spirit, meaning that one should so yield to the Spirit that one's entire being is enlightened and governed by Him. In the 20th century, theologians like Dietrich Bonhoeffer (though we will not quote him here, as he was cited earlier) warned of "cheap grace" – the notion that one could have justification without sanctification. Bonhoeffer insisted that "only he who believes is obedient, and only he who is obedient believes," highlighting that genuine faith involves a life of discipleship and cross-bearing. Likewise, Dallas Willard observed that accepting Christ's invitation means becoming His apprentice in kingdom living – learning to live as He lived.

Though Willard has been referenced previously, it is worth noting his insight that spiritual formation is unavoidable: everyone is being formed by something; the question is whether we are being conformed to Christ or to the patterns of the world. The consensus of Christian tradition is that to be a Christian is to be changing. If there is no evidence of growth in grace or increase in holiness, something is amiss. Jesus said that a tree is known by its fruit; likewise, a Christ-follower is known by an increasingly Christlike character. This does not mean Christians never stumble or that growth is linear. There are ups and downs, seasons of rapid progress and seasons of struggle. But over the long arc of life, those who belong to Jesus will be "transformed...from one degree of glory to another" by the Spirit's work. This transformation is a testimony to the world of the reality of Christ's power, and it has been the mark of true saints in every age.

One beautiful historical example of prioritizing transformation is seen in the life of the 19th-century Scottish pastor Robert Murray McCheyne. Renowned for his personal piety, McCheyne once said, "The greatest need of my people is my personal holiness."[54] In other words, more than eloquent sermons or efficient programs, what his congregation needed most was a pastor who was Christlike in character. This statement reflects a deep understanding that holy character has a profound impact on others. McCheyne knew that if he embodied the love and purity of Christ, it would speak more loudly than any words. His conviction has echoed through time as a challenge to every Christian: one of the best gifts we can give to the world is our own transformation. When we are changed – even partially – into the likeness of Jesus, we become channels of God's presence and blessing to those around us.

Habits and Spiritual Disciplines that Foster Inner Transformation

If Christlike character is the destination, how do we get there? While the Holy Spirit is the primary agent of transformation, Christians through the ages have identified various practices – often called spiritual disciplines or means of grace – that position us to receive God's transforming work. These habits, grounded in Scripture and modeled by Jesus and the apostles, create space in our lives for the Holy Spirit to shape us. As the saying goes, we "cannot change ourselves, but we can

---

[54] Kevin DeYoung, "The Pastor's Personal Holiness," *The Gospel Coalition* (blog), July 23, 2015

put ourselves in the path of the divine change-agent." The disciplines are like tools that till the soil of our hearts so that the "seed" of God's Word and Spirit can bear fruit (cf. Gal. 6:7–8).[55] Below are some key practices and how they cultivate Christlike character:

- **Prayer:** A life of regular prayer is indispensable to transformation. Prayer is both communion with God and communication that changes us. In prayer we adore God (which cultivates love and reverence), we confess sin (fostering humility and honesty), we give thanks (breeding gratitude), and we bring requests (growing our trust and dependence). Richard Foster calls prayer "the most central of the disciplines because it ushers us into perpetual communion with the Father."[56] Through daily prayer – whether in private devotions, praying Scripture (like the Psalms), or continual "breath prayers" throughout the day – our hearts are realigned toward God. Over time, a praying Christian becomes a peaceful and God-centered Christian, reflecting Christ's own prayerful reliance on the Father. Jesus Himself often withdrew to solitary places to pray, sometimes spending whole nights in prayer (Luke 5:16; Mark 1:35). If the Son of God lived in such prayer, how much more do we need prayer as the furnace that warms and softens our hearts for God's work?

- **Scripture Meditation and Study:** Jesus said, "Man shall not live by bread alone, but by every word that comes

---

[55] Richard J. Foster, *Celebration of Discipline: The Path to Spiritual Growth* (San Francisco: Harper & Row, 1978), 2.
[56] Ibid., 33

from the mouth of God" (Matt. 4:4). The Word of God is food for our souls and a primary instrument of our sanctification (John 17:17). Studying the Bible renews our minds and corrects false thinking, while meditating on Scripture (slowly, prayerfully internalizing it) implants truth deep within us. For example, regularly meditating on Jesus' teachings in the Sermon on the Mount will gradually shape our values to mirror the kingdom (Matt. 5–7). The Psalmist declared, "I have stored up your word in my heart, that I might not sin against you" (Ps. 119:11). Memorizing and pondering Scripture arms us with Christ's mindset when we face temptation or decisions. Practically, disciplines like *lectio divina* (sacred reading) help believers read the Bible and listen to God through it, leading to personal transformation. Through Scripture, we behold the glory of the Lord and are changed (2 Cor. 3:18). The Bible also acts as a mirror to show us where we fall short and need to repent (James 1:22–25). A Christlike character cannot be formed apart from the continual intake of God's Word.

- **Silence and Solitude:** In our noisy, busy world, the disciplines of silence and solitude are often neglected but extremely powerful. Reflecting on the wisdom of the Desert Fathers, Henri Nouwen wrote, "Solitude is the furnace of transformation. Without solitude, we remain victims of our society and continue to be entangled in the illusions of the false self."[57] Stepping away regularly from the hustle of life – whether for an hour, a day, or

---

[57] Henri J. M. Nouwen, *The Way of the Heart: Desert Spirituality and Contemporary Ministry* (New York: Seabury Press, 1981), 15

longer retreats – allows us to confront our inner life honestly before God. In solitude, distractions are removed, and the Holy Spirit can reveal areas in our hearts that need change (anger, pride, wounds, etc.). Silence before God trains us to listen rather than always speak, cultivating a humble, receptive spirit. Jesus Himself spent forty days in the wilderness before beginning His ministry, facing temptation in solitude and emerging empowered by the Spirit (Luke 4:1–14). Likewise, many mature Christians testify that periods of quiet withdrawal for prayer, reflection, and simply being with God have marked turning points in their spiritual growth. In a culture of constant stimulation, choosing silence can break the addiction to noise and activity, allowing us to hear God's gentle voice and find our identity in Him rather than in doing.

- **Fasting:** Fasting, the voluntary abstention from food (or something else like media) for a time, is a classic discipline to humble ourselves and seek God. Fasting reveals how much our appetites rule us and teaches us self-control and reliance on God. By saying "no" to the body's cravings for a period, we declare that God is our ultimate sustainer, not bread alone. This can break the power of gluttony, lust, or consumerism in us. Moreover, fasting often brings inner struggles – irritability, impatience – to the surface, which we can then surrender to Christ for transformation. Biblically, people fasted as they repented of sin, sought guidance, or interceded for others. Jesus assumed His followers would fast (Matt. 6:16–18) and modeled it during His 40-day wilderness fast. While fasting can be challenging, its fruit is a greater mastery over self and a more intense focus on God. It also increases our empathy for the hungry and needy, thus building compassion. When combined with prayer and Scripture, fasting can significantly deepen one's spiritual life and accelerate growth in holiness, as we learn that "my food is to do the will of Him who sent me" (John 4:34).

- **Obedience and Service:** Sometimes overlooked as "disciplines," the simple practices of obeying God's promptings and serving others are actually among the most transformative. Each time we obey God's Word – whether in a moral choice (e.g., telling the truth instead of a lie) or responding to the Spirit's nudge (e.g., encouraging someone or giving generously) – we strengthen Christlike character. Obedience, repeated over time, forms holy habits. Jesus emphasized faithfulness in the small things (Luke 16:10). As we consistently choose integrity, purity, and kindness in the mundane moments, these virtues become "second nature." Similarly, actively serving others in love has a purifying effect on our souls. Jesus came "not to be served, but to serve" (Mark 10:45), and when we take on the role of a servant – whether through volunteering, helping the poor, or simply putting a neighbor's needs before our own – we crucify our selfishness and let Christ's humility grow in us. Service is a discipline of action that trains us to look not only to our own interests but also to the interests of others (Phil. 2:4–5). It delivers a blow to pride and teaches practical love. Many Christians can attest that seasons of dedicated service (missions, caring for a sick family member, etc.) considerably stretched and transformed their character, making them more patient, compassionate, and reliant on God. Obedience and service also guard us from the deception of knowledge without practice. As James 1:22 reminds us, we must "be doers of the word, and not hearers only." In doing so, we are changed.

- **Community and Confession:** Transformation is not a lone project; God often uses community to shape us. Regular fellowship with other believers – in corporate worship, small groups, spiritual friendships – provides accountability, encouragement, and sometimes loving rebuke that spurs growth. Proverbs 27:17 says, "As iron sharpens iron, so one person sharpens another." Being committed to a church community challenges us to practice forgiveness, bear with others' weaknesses, and receive grace ourselves. One specific communal discipline is confession – openly admitting our sins or struggles to God before others (e.g., to a pastor or prayer partner). Confession humbles us and breaks the power of secret sin, paving the way for healing (James 5:16). The early church practiced confessing sins to one another and praying for each other, knowing this fostered holiness. In a trustworthy community, we can take off our masks, and our darkness begins to dissipate in that light. Community also allows us to see Christlike examples up close and imitate their faith (Heb. 13:7). Simply put, we grow better together. God often uses the friction and affection of relationships to sand off our rough edges and inspire us onward.

Other disciplines could be mentioned – worship, Sabbath rest, simplicity, journaling, and more – but the pattern is that these practices create channels for God's transforming grace. Importantly, we must remember that the disciplines themselves do not transform us; God transforms us by His grace, but the disciplines position us to receive that grace. As Richard Foster writes, "The purpose of the spiritual disciplines is the total transformation of the person"[58] – they help replace old, destructive habits with new, life-giving habits oriented toward God. By consistently practicing such habits, we cooperate with the Holy Spirit's work in us.

Over time, our external routines become internalized virtues. For example, a person who regularly practices generosity (even when it is hard) finds that they gradually become generous-hearted. One who disciplines themselves to bless those who curse them finds that, in time, Christ's love for enemies has taken root in their heart. In short, we cultivate Christlike character by cultivating Christlike practices. As we do so, we must rely on God at every step, for apart from Christ we can do nothing (John 15:5). But with Him, we can do all things – including grow into His likeness (Phil. 4:13).

Common Obstacles to Spiritual Transformation

If growing in Christlikeness is the call, why do so many struggle or stall in this process? Transformation is complex; we must recognize and overcome various obstacles and oppositions with God's help. Awareness of these common pitfalls can help us navigate or break through them. Here are several significant obstacles to spiritual transformation and how to address them:

---

[58] Foster, *Celebration of Discipline*, 2

- **Pride:** Throughout Christian history, pride has been identified as the deadliest spiritual vice – "the essential vice, the utmost evil," as C.S. Lewis put it.[59] Pride is the exaltation of self, the attitude that says "I know best" or "I deserve glory." It resists transformation because it resists submission, and transformation requires submitting to God's will and correction. A proud heart does not readily admit fault or need, short-circuits repentance (a key growth driver). Pride was the original sin that turned Lucifer into the devil, and it "leads to every other vice" by making us self-centered.[60] If we are convinced of our goodness or strength, we will not seek God's grace to change. Therefore, combating pride is critical. God often humbles us through circumstances or failures to bring us to a place where we genuinely cry, "Teach me, Lord; change me." Practicing disciplines of humility – such as confession, serving in hidden ways, and intentionally listening to others – can help break pride's grip. Regularly gazing at the glory and holiness of God in Scripture and prayer will also shrink our ego as we, like Isaiah, exclaim "Woe is me" and then receive God's cleansing (Isa.. 6:5–7). In contrast to pride, humility opens the door wide for transformation, because "God opposes the proud but gives grace to the humble" (James 4:6). When we humble ourselves, we become teachable clay in the Potter's hands.

- **Apathy and Sloth:** Another subtle but serious obstacle is spiritual laziness or apathy – historically called *acedia* or

---

[59] C. S. Lewis, *Mere Christianity* (New York: HarperCollins, 2001), 122
[60] Ibid., 123

sloth. This is a condition of the heart in which one loses motivation for the things of God. The early monks spoke of acedia as the "noonday demon" that would make a monk restless or indifferent to prayer and work midway through the day. In modern terms, a Christian might experience this as a spiritual doldrums – a season where one feels "stuck," bored, or simply unmotivated to pursue growth. Apathy can creep in through complacency (thinking "I am good enough as I am") or through discouragement (feeling "I will never change, so why try?"). It can also be fueled by the constant distractions of entertainment and digital media that induce a passive, numb state. Sloth is dangerous because transformation requires intentionality and effort (again, not in our own strength alone, but cooperative effort with God). If we do nothing, we tend to drift away from Christlikeness, not toward it. Sometimes we must engage in disciplined action to overcome apathy, even when our feelings are cold, trusting that desire often follows discipline. As the author of Hebrews urges, "lift your drooping hands and strengthen your weak knees" (Heb. 12:12). Pushing through dry spells in prayer or Scripture reading eventually yields fruit as God honors persistence. Also, meeting with fervent believers can rekindle our zeal (Heb. 10:24–25). Ultimately, we combat sloth by remembering the worth of Christ and the stakes of our calling. We preach to our souls that "it is time to seek the Lord" (Hos. 10:12) and ask the Spirit to set us ablaze anew. God is gracious to revive the heart of the contrite and sluggish when we repent of our complacency.

- **Cultural Conformity:** The broader culture exerts a powerful shaping force on our character – often in ways contrary to Christ. If we passively imbibe the values and norms of the world around us, we will be "conformed to this age" (Rom. 12:2) rather than transformed to God's will. Today's culture prizes things like self-indulgence, materialism, sexual libertinism, and radical individualism – all of which conflict with the way of Christ (which calls for self-denial, generosity, purity, and community). One common obstacle is the sheer busyness and noise of modern life. We are so over-occupied and overstimulated that we have little bandwidth for God. As a result, our spiritual growth can be choked out like seed among thorns (Mark 4:19). Another aspect is the influence of secular ideologies and media that shape our thinking more than Scripture does. If we binge on social media, news, and entertainment but only nibble on God's Word, our worldview and character will reflect the world more than the kingdom. Overcoming cultural conformity requires a degree of holy resistance – making conscious choices that may seem counter-cultural. This might mean simplifying our lifestyle, limiting media consumption, observing a weekly Sabbath rest, or valuing relationship over productivity to create space for God's transforming work. It also means renewing the mind continuously with biblical truth to discern where culture's ideas must be rejected or redeemed. Christian transformation often involves a "detox" from worldly patterns as we take on the "culture of Christ." The pressure to fit in with society can be intense (whether in moral compromises or chasing status), but Romans 12:2 gives the strategy: refuse conformity and pursue inner renewal. When we remember that we are citizens of heaven (Phil. 3:20) and pilgrims on earth, we can hold the world's pressures loosely and follow Jesus' higher call.

- **Ungodly Attachments and Idols:** Another internal obstacle is the presence of idols in the heart – things or desires we love more than God, which hinder our spiritual progress. These can be overt sins or even good things that have become inordinate. For example, one might be a Christian yet secretly be enslaved to greed, or lust, or the approval of others. These attachments function like spiritual "weights" that slow our race (Heb. 12:1). As long as we cling to a particular sin or even an otherwise legitimate pleasure that we refuse to surrender, our growth will be stunted at that point. Jesus said, "Where your treasure is, there your heart will be also" (Matt. 6:21). If our treasure is not Christ above all, our heart will not fully belong to Him for transformation. Dealing with idols often involves painful but necessary surrender. We might need to cut off a habit, relationship, or ambition that competes with God. This can feel like losing part of oneself – and indeed Jesus likened it to gouging out an eye or cutting off a hand to avoid sin (Matt. 5:29–30). However, the Spirit's power can free us from enslaving attachments. One encouraging strategy is the "expulsive power of a new affection," a phrase from the preacher Thomas Chalmers. Rather than only attempting to uproot the idol (negative), we plant a stronger love for Christ (positive) in our hearts, eventually displacing the lesser love. The more we see Jesus as supremely beautiful and satisfying, the less grip our idols will have. Thus, worship and meditating on God's goodness are crucial in idol-breaking. Additionally, accountability with a mature believer or counselor can help us name and dismantle our personal idols, whether it be addictions, prideful ambition, or something like an identity apart from Christ. Liberation from idols brings a rush of new growth, as the energy being diverted to them is now available to propel us toward God.

- **Discouragement and Guilt:** Many Christians begin the journey of transformation with zeal, only to falter when they encounter their own repeated failures. The process of sanctification can be slow and often takes two steps forward and one step back. In battling long-entrenched sins or habits, we may fall multiple times. At such points, discouragement becomes a real enemy. We might think, "I am not getting any better," and be tempted to give up. The devil (called the accuser in Rev. 12:10) loves to use false guilt or shame to make us believe we are unworthy and incapable of change. Excessive introspection can also lead to despair if we focus more on our sin than our Savior. To overcome this obstacle, we must keep our eyes on Christ's sufficiency rather than our insufficiency. Remembering truths like "There is no condemnation for those in Christ Jesus" (Rom. 8:1) and "He who began a good work in you will bring it to completion" (Phil. 1:6) fortifies us to continue. We should normalize that growth often comes with setbacks and that God's grace is greater than our sin. As John Newton aptly said, "I am not what I ought to be, I am not what I want to be, but still I am not what I once used to be, and by the grace of God I am what I am." Celebrating incremental progress, however small, and practicing quick repentance and re-acceptance of God's forgiveness will keep us moving forward. It is also vital to draw encouragement from the testimonies of others and from Scripture's promises. When weary, recall Isaiah 40:31: "They who wait for the Lord shall renew their strength... they shall run and not be weary." Perseverance is itself a Christlike virtue, and overcoming discouragement to continue the race will, in retrospect, be one of the ways God makes us more like Jesus (who, for the joy set before Him, endured the cross, Heb. 12:2).

In confronting each obstacle – pride, apathy, worldliness, idolatry, discouragement, and more – the overarching key is repeatedly returning to the gospel of grace. The gospel reminds us that we are not accepted because we are already righteous; we are accepted because of Christ's righteousness. Therefore, we can face our faults without fear, knowing His blood covers them. The gospel also reminds us that the same power that raised Jesus from the dead is at work in us (Eph. 1:19–20). No chain is too complex for God to break, and no nature is too complex for Him to change. Hope in God's promises is a potent antidote to every obstacle. As we cling to His Word – "My grace is sufficient for you, for My power is made perfect in weakness" (2 Cor. 12:9) – we find strength to lay aside every weight and sin and run with endurance. Every obstacle overcome becomes a stepping stone toward greater maturity. In fact, many saints testify that their seasons of struggle or opposition became the context in which God forged Christlike virtues (for example, patience through trials, faith through silence, humility through failure). God in His providence even uses obstacles for our transformation, as we yield them to Him.

Conclusion: The Necessity of Christlikeness for Kingdom Impact

In the grand scheme of God's redemptive plan, becoming like Christ is not an optional pursuit for the especially devout – it is the essence of our salvation. The New Testament vision is that the church would be a community of people who think, feel, and act like Jesus did, thereby continuing His presence and mission in the world. This stage of Transformation in the believer's life is therefore critical for the sake of the Kingdom of God. Jesus taught that His followers are the "salt of the earth" and the "light of the world" (Matt. 5:13–16). However, what gives salt its saltiness and light its brightness? It is the distinctive character of Christ within us. A worldly, selfish, or immature Christian cannot effectively witness to a holy, loving Christ. Conversely, a believer whose life radiates the compassion, purity, and integrity of Jesus becomes a beacon that draws others to God. When we are Christlike, our lives validate the gospel message we proclaim. People may debate our doctrine, but cannot easily dismiss a life transformed by grace into one of humble love.

Cultivating Christlike character is also essential for our specific callings and ministries. Whatever spiritual gifts or talents we have, it is Christlike character that ensures those gifts are exercised in a godly manner. For example, a person might have the gift of teaching, but without patience, gentleness, and love (all fruit of the Spirit), that teaching can become harsh or prideful and do harm. Character is the foundation that carries the weight of our gifts. This is why the apostle Paul, when listing qualifications for church leaders, focuses almost entirely on mature character traits (1 Tim. 3:1–7). God's work through us will only be as deep as His work in us. Allowing God to refine and mold our inner life is non-negotiable if we long to significantly impact God's Kingdom—whether in our family, community, or world. A famous saying attributed to Robert Murray McCheyne bears repeating: "My people's greatest need is my personal holiness."[61] The world's greatest need is Jesus, and they see Jesus in us most clearly when walking in His holiness and love. A holy, united in love, and merciful church will starkly contrast to the darkness, and "then the world will know" that Jesus truly saves (cf. John 13:35; 17:21).

Ultimately, becoming like Christ is necessary not only for effective witness but for the very glory of God. Jesus said, "By this my Father is glorified, that you bear much fruit and so prove to be my disciples" (John 15:8, ESV). When the character of Christ—His goodness, kindness, purity, and love—is evident in us, God is glorified, because it is His work on display. Our transformation is a trophy of His grace. We show the world what God can do with broken, selfish people: He can recreate them to shine with the likeness of His Son. There is no greater miracle. In fact, Ephesians 2:10 calls us God's workmanship (*poiēma*, His masterpiece), created in Christ for good works. The transformation of sinners into saints is like a spiritual art piece that God is crafting through the ages, something that will redound to His praise forever. This perspective helps us see why transformation is so central: it is part of God's joy in redemption to see His children reflect His image freely. As any parent delights to see their child grow in wisdom and virtue, our

---

[61] 1 Kevin DeYoung, "The Pastor's Personal Holiness," *The Gospel Coalition* (blog), July 23, 2015.

heavenly Father rejoices over each step of our growth in Christlikeness.

In conclusion, Stage 2 of the Christian journey – Transformation: Cultivating Christlike Character – is both a divine gift and a divine summons. It is God's gift that He does not leave us as we were, but by the Holy Spirit, can change even the hardest heart. Moreover, it is God's summons that we actively pursue this change, working out our salvation and putting on the Lord Jesus in every area of life. Theologically, we have seen that transformation is grounded in our union with Christ and enabled by the Spirit, with deep roots in biblical revelation. Historically, we stand on the shoulders of saints who have blazed the trail of holiness and given us wisdom on running this race. Practically, we have myriad tools at our disposal – spiritual disciplines and habits of grace – to till the soil of our hearts for growth. Moreover, realistically, we know there will be obstacles, but we are armed with awareness and God's promises to overcome them.

Let us therefore embrace this glorious calling to become like our Master. In doing so, we honor the One who loved us and gave Himself for us. We also prepare ourselves to carry out His mission – because the world desperately needs Christ-like Christians: people who forgive as He forgave, who speak truth with love, who serve selflessly, who pursue justice with mercy, who exhibit calm faith in trials, and who love even their enemies. Such people truly "shine as lights in the world" (Phil. 2:15). The degree to which we allow Christ to transform us is the degree to which our lives can impact a Kingdom. Indeed, our transformation is Kingdom impact, for wherever a life becomes more aligned with heaven, the reign of God is breaking through.

May we, by God's grace, continue on this transformative journey with hope and perseverance. As we do, we can trust that Jesus Himself is with us as both model and empowerer – the author and finisher of our faith (Heb. 12:2). He will see us through to completion, and one day we will stand before Him, fully transformed, and hear, "Well done, good and faithful servant." That eternal moment will make every effort worth it. Until then, let us press on to become like Christ, for God's glory and the world's sake.

Chapter 7

Persevere in the Journey: Endurance and the Sustaining Presence of God.

Inner resilience and perseverance are vital attributes that characterize spiritual maturity and Christlike virtue. Believers will face many trials and challenging moments throughout their spiritual journeys, yet their steadfast endurance and unwavering trust in God's providential care reveal their true faith. The Scriptures repeatedly affirm that perseverance in the face of adversity leads to deeper spiritual maturity and ultimate blessings, promising a reward for steadfast endurance: "Blessed is the one who perseveres under trial because, having stood the test, that person will receive the crown of life that the Lord has promised to those who love him" (James 1:12, NIV).

This chapter extensively examines the theological underpinnings, historical examples, biblical precedents, practical spiritual disciplines, and common challenges related to cultivating inner resilience and perseverance. Throughout, we will explore how enduring faith is both a gift from God and a discipline cultivated through life's tests, aiming to equip the believer with understanding and practice for a resilient walk with Christ.

Theological Foundations

Theologically, resilience and perseverance are integral components of the Christian doctrine of sanctification. The sanctification process involves the transformation of believers into the likeness of Christ, a transformation that often occurs through trials and tribulations. Apostle Paul explicitly details this sanctifying process: "We also glory in our sufferings, because we know that suffering produces perseverance; perseverance, character; and character, hope" (Rom. 5:3–4, NIV). Here, perseverance transcends mere endurance and becomes a powerful mechanism through which God shapes believers' character and deepens their reliance on His sovereign purposes. As J.I. Packer noted, "Perseverance is the product of a faith refined by suffering, a hope anchored in the promises of God."[62]

Perseverance is also grounded in the doctrine of divine providence, which affirms God's active role in guiding and sustaining the believer's journey. This understanding assures believers that their suffering is not meaningless but is used by God for redemptive purposes. God's providential oversight is vividly expressed in Romans 8:28, which promises that "in all things God works for the good of those who love him, who have been called according to his purpose."

Additionally, perseverance aligns closely with the doctrinal concept of the perseverance of the saints, highlighting God's unwavering commitment to preserve His people through various trials. Hebrews 12:1–2 uses the vivid metaphor of a race to urge believers toward resilience: "run with perseverance the

---

[62] J.I. Packer, Knowing God (Downers Grove, IL: InterVarsity Press, 1973), 231

race marked out for us, fixing our eyes on Jesus, the pioneer and perfecter of faith." Jesus Himself personifies ultimate resilience, enduring extreme suffering and the shame of the cross, setting a profound example for all believers to follow (Heb. 12:2).

Moreover, resilience is deeply rooted in the biblical understanding of hope. Paul teaches that true Christian hope does not disappoint because it is grounded in God's unchanging love and faithfulness (Rom. 5:5). This theological perspective underscores the certainty of God's promises, providing believers with unwavering confidence that empowers their perseverance through trials.

A key aspect of theological reflection on resilience is the eschatological hope that motivates believers to endure present suffering in anticipation of future glory. Paul writes in 2 Corinthians 4:17, "For our light and momentary troubles are achieving for us an eternal glory that far outweighs them all." This eternal perspective encourages believers to remain faithful, knowing that their trials are temporary and purposeful.

Finally, resilience is nurtured through participation in the life of the Spirit. Galatians 5:22–23 lists patience and self-control—qualities essential to resilience—as fruit of the Spirit. The Spirit empowers believers not only to endure but to grow through suffering. The Spirit sustains, strengthens, and shapes believers into the image of Christ amid adversity.

Together, these theological principles establish a robust framework for understanding resilience and perseverance not merely as human efforts but as divinely enabled virtues that play a critical role in the believer's sanctification and witness to the world.

Biblical Exemplars of Resilience

Scripture presents numerous examples of individuals who embodied remarkable perseverance while under pressure, hardship, and injustice. These historical figures are not merely historical characters but theological exemplars whose lives offer guidance and encouragement to contemporary believers.

Job remains the quintessential example of endurance through profound suffering. Though he lost his wealth, health, and children, Job maintained a persistent, though anguished, trust in God. His statement, "Though he slay me, yet will I hope in him" (Job 13:15), expresses a defiant hope that anchors faith amidst chaos. Job's eventual restoration serves as personal vindication and a theological affirmation of God's faithfulness to the persevering. [63]

Joseph, sold by his brothers and imprisoned unjustly in Egypt, demonstrates resilience marked by trust, integrity, and forgiveness. Despite years of suffering, he declared, "You intended to harm me, but God intended it for good" (Gen. 50:20). Joseph's narrative reveals a theology of providence—how divine purposes unfold even through human wrongdoing—and showcases a resilience that results in reconciliation and generational salvation. [64]

David, pursued by Saul and plagued by personal failings, regularly turned to God in raw, honest prayer. The Psalms reflect a resilient soul that continually returns to God for strength, even

---

[63] Robert Alter, The Art of Biblical Narrative (New York: Basic Books, 1981).

[64] John Goldingay, Old Testament Theology: Israel's Gospel (Downers Grove, IL: IVP Academic, 2003)

after sin or despair. David's resilience includes enduring external threats and internal battles, teaching that spiritual perseverance includes repentance and restoration.[65]

The Apostle Paul is perhaps the most vivid New Testament example of resilience. Beaten, shipwrecked, imprisoned, and opposed, Paul continued to preach the gospel with fervor. His letters often reflect a theology shaped in suffering: "I have learned to be content whatever the circumstances... I can do all this through him who gives me strength" (Phil. 4:11–13). Paul's view of resilience is deeply Christocentric, interpreting his trials as participation in the sufferings of Christ (Phil. 3:10).[66]

Jesus Christ, above all, exemplifies perfect endurance. He was "a man of sorrows, acquainted with grief" (Isa. 53:3), yet He remained obedient unto death. His struggle in Gethsemane and declaration on the cross—"It is finished" (John 19:30)—underscores that true resilience is ultimately about faithfulness to God's will. Jesus endured to model perseverance and make it possible for others.[67]

Nehemiah, facing ridicule, opposition, and internal discouragement while rebuilding Jerusalem's wall, displayed leadership resilience rooted in prayer and purpose. He declared, "The joy of the Lord is your strength" (Neh. 8:10), a reminder

---

[65] Timothy Keller, Walking with God through Pain and Suffering (New York: Penguin Books, 2015).
[66] Gordon D. Fee, Paul, the Spirit, and the People of God (Peabody, MA: Hendrickson, 1996).
[67] N. T. Wright, The Day the Revolution Began: Reconsidering the Meaning of Jesus's Crucifixion (San Francisco: HarperOne, 2016).

that communal perseverance arises from divine joy, not human grit.[68]

Each figure—Job, Joseph, David, Paul, Nehemiah, and Christ—embodies different facets of resilience. Together, they form a composite picture of faithful endurance. Their lives invite believers today to emulate their trust in God, their tenacity in adversity, and their hope in divine purposes that transcend present pain.

Historical Insights on Perseverance

Historically, believers have consistently demonstrated perseverance amid persecution, hardship, and systemic oppression. These historical insights inspire and serve as theological reflections on how divine grace enables long-term endurance.

Christian martyrs like Polycarp and Perpetua embodied profound spiritual resilience in the early church. Polycarp's refusal to renounce Christ, even under threat of death by fire, revealed his deep conviction and trust in eternal life. According to *The Martyrdom of Polycarp*, his final words were a doxology of unwavering faith: "Eighty-six years I have served Him, and He has done me no wrong. How then can I blaspheme my King and Savior?"[69] These martyrdom accounts became foundational narratives for early Christians, reinforcing the belief that suffering for Christ was honorable and redemptive.

---

[68] Dietrich Bonhoeffer, Letters and Papers from Prison (New York: Touchstone, 1997).

[69] J.B. Lightfoot and J.R. Harmer, The Apostolic Fathers (Grand Rapids, MI: Baker Book House, 1989).

During the medieval period, monastic movements offered another form of perseverance marked by disciplined spiritual practice. Monks such as Benedict of Nursia developed rules of life that emphasized prayer, manual labor, and communal living. The *Rule of St. Benedict* famously encourages stability and obedience as spiritual disciplines that cultivate inner strength and consistency in one's vocation.[70] Such practices reflected a theology that equated perseverance with enduring persecution and patient, lifelong fidelity.

The Protestant Reformation introduced fresh theological emphasis on perseverance as a manifestation of saving faith. Despite excommunication threats and personal struggles, Martin Luther proclaimed, "Here I stand; I can do no other." His doctrine of justification by faith insisted that true faith would inevitably lead to perseverance in righteousness.[71] Similarly, John Calvin articulated the doctrine of the "perseverance of the saints," asserting that God's elect, preserved by divine grace, would endure.[72] This doctrinal emphasis assured believers that perseverance was a gift and a sign of authentic salvation.

In the modern era, figures like Dietrich Bonhoeffer and Corrie ten Boom demonstrated resilience in the face of Nazi oppression. Bonhoeffer's writings from prison reflect a deeply forged faith that interpreted suffering through Christ's own obedience. He wrote, "The ultimate test of a moral society is the

---

[70] St. Benedict, The Rule of St. Benedict, trans. Timothy Fry (Collegeville, MN: Liturgical Press, 1981).
[71] Martin Luther, The Freedom of a Christian, trans. Mark Tranvik (Minneapolis, MN: Fortress Press, 2008).
[72] John Calvin, Institutes of the Christian Religion, ed. John T. McNeill, trans. Ford Lewis Battles (Philadelphia: Westminster Press, 1960).

kind of world it leaves to its children."[73] Corrie ten Boom, a Dutch Christian who helped Jews escape the Holocaust, later emphasized forgiveness and hope despite enduring a concentration camp. Her testimony in *The Hiding Place* underscores how faith enables forgiveness, even in the aftermath of evil.[74]

These historical accounts demonstrate that perseverance is not a new Christian ideal but a deeply embedded virtue across the ages. Whether through martyrdom, monasticism, reformation, or resistance, the faithful have testified that God's sustaining grace empowers believers to endure, flourish, and witness—often in the darkest times.

Practical Disciplines for Building Resilience

Spiritual resilience is not merely developed through passive waiting during trials—it must be intentionally cultivated through practical disciplines that anchor the soul in God. These disciplines, grounded in Scripture and affirmed through church tradition, serve as preventative and restorative practices that nurture inner strength.

1. Prayer as Daily Anchoring

Prayer is the foundational spiritual discipline that aligns the believer's heart with God's presence and purposes. In seasons of difficulty, it becomes the lifeline that sustains faith and hope. Jesus modeled a persistent prayer life, often retreating to solitary places to commune with the Father (Luke 5:16). Through prayer,

---

[73] Dietrich Bonhoeffer, Ethics, trans. Clifford J. Green (Minneapolis, MN: Fortress Press, 2005).
[74] Corrie ten Boom, The Hiding Place (Grand Rapids, MI: Chosen Books, 1971).

believers pour out their fears and frustrations while receiving divine strength to endure. Structured prayer times, such as fixed-hour prayer or the Daily Office, provide consistent touchpoints with God that shape resilience through rhythm and trust.

2. Scriptural Immersion and Meditation

Engaging the Word of God is essential for building spiritual endurance. Paul described Scripture as "God-breathed and useful for teaching, rebuking, correcting and training in righteousness" (2 Tim. 3:16). Memorizing, meditating on, and internalizing Scripture forms a reservoir of truth that believers can draw upon in times of adversity. Psalms of lament, like Psalm 13 or 42, provide language for grief, while narratives of perseverance offer inspiration and reassurance.

3. Worship and Gratitude Practices

Worship reorients the believer's perspective from circumstances to the sovereignty of God. In Acts 16, Paul and Silas sang hymns in prison, demonstrating that praise in hardship can transform atmospheres and inner attitudes. Similarly, the discipline of gratitude, even in trial, cultivates a posture of resilience. Keeping a gratitude journal, intentionally thanking God in prayer, and participating in communal worship fortify spiritual resolve.

4. Sabbath and Rest

Resilience requires margin. The discipline of Sabbath offers rest for the soul and a reminder that God is ultimately in control. Sabbath observance allows space for reflection, emotional recalibration, and spiritual renewal. Jesus' invitation to the weary in Matthew 11:28–30—"Come to me, all you who are weary and burdened, and I will give you rest"—emphasizes that resilience is strengthened, not weakened, through rest in Him.

5. Community and Accountability

Spiritual resilience is not a solitary endeavor. The early church exemplified mutual encouragement and shared endurance (Acts 2:42–47). Small groups, spiritual friendships, and mentoring relationships serve as support systems that uphold believers in times of struggle. James 5:16 exhorts, "Confess your sins to each other and pray for each other so that you may be healed." Regular connection with trusted believers cultivates resilience through empathy, prayer, and shared wisdom.

6. Fasting and Surrender

Fasting trains the believer to deny the flesh and lean into divine strength. It is both a declaration of dependence and a practice of purification. In moments of challenge, fasting clarifies focus, reveals hidden dependencies, and fosters humility. Jesus began His ministry with fasting (Matt. 4:1–11), revealing that spiritual stamina is often forged through intentional sacrifice.

7. Journaling and Reflective Writing

Reflective practices such as journaling provide a space to process pain, record God's faithfulness, and trace spiritual growth. Lamentations, David's psalms, and the confessions of early church fathers all mirror this practice. Writing becomes a spiritual mirror and a tool for resilience, documenting how God meets believers in their darkest valleys.

Together, these disciplines form a spiritual training regimen. They are not emergency measures but lifelong habits that prepare the heart to remain steadfast through storms. Just as physical resilience requires consistent exercise and nourishment, so does spiritual resilience demand daily practices that fix the believer's gaze on Christ, the One who endured the cross and now sustains His people with unshakeable grace.

Overcoming Obstacles to Resilience

While Scripture and spiritual tradition offer powerful resources for cultivating resilience, believers must also recognize and confront the real-world obstacles that hinder the development of perseverance. The challenges of modern life, spiritual warfare, and internal conflicts often conspire to weaken resolve and discourage consistent growth. Overcoming these barriers requires discernment, grace, and intentionality.

1. Cultural Messages of Instant Gratification

Modern society is built around immediacy—fast results, quick solutions, and instant comfort. This mindset directly opposes the biblical call to endurance, which often requires waiting, persistence, and unseen progress. The constant exposure to messages that promise quick fixes can lead to impatience and spiritual restlessness. Christians must reframe their expectations, learning to value long obedience in the same direction. Romans 5:3–4 reminds us that "suffering produces perseverance; perseverance, character; and character, hope."

2. Emotional Fatigue and Burnout

A significant obstacle to resilience is emotional exhaustion. Many believers face relentless pressures—work demands, family responsibilities, ministry expectations—that leave little room for rest. When the soul is depleted, perseverance becomes increasingly tricky. Elijah's story in 1 Kings 19 illustrates this point well: after his great spiritual victory at Mount Carmel, he experienced deep despair and wished for death. God's response was tender care—providing sleep, food, and stillness. Believers must give themselves permission to rest and receive restoration.

3. Spiritual Apathy and Disconnection

In seasons of hardship, some believers grow cold in their faith, either from prolonged unanswered prayers or disappointment with God's timing. Spiritual apathy—a loss of fervor or hunger for God—erodes the will to persevere. Hebrews 10:36 encourages us, "You need to persevere so that when you have done the will of God, you will receive what he has promised." Spiritual renewal often begins with small steps—re-engaging in prayer, Scripture reading, or joining fellowship—to reignite the flame of devotion.

4. Fear of Failure or Weakness

The fear of not measuring up can be paralyzing. Believers may hide their vulnerabilities when resilience is perceived as never struggling or being perpetually strong. However, Scripture is clear that God's strength is made perfect in weakness (2 Cor. 12:9). True resilience is not about perfection but about surrender—acknowledging dependence on the Holy Spirit, leaning on others in community, and trusting God's grace to sustain through every valley.

5. Isolation from Community

Loneliness is a breeding ground for discouragement. In times of testing, isolation amplifies despair. The enemy often targets believers by cutting them off from life-giving relationships. Ecclesiastes 4:9–10 teaches that "two are better than one" because they can support and lift one another. A practical step in overcoming this obstacle is engaging in small groups, accountability partnerships, or mentoring relationships that nurture spiritual resilience.

6. The Lies of the Enemy

Satan's primary tactic is deception—whispering lies that God is distant, that failure defines identity, or that the struggle is hopeless. These accusations, if left unchecked, sap spiritual strength. Ephesians 6:16 exhorts believers to take up "the shield of faith, with which you can extinguish all the flaming arrows of the evil one." Overcoming spiritual attacks requires immersion in truth, declarations of faith, and prayerful resistance.

7. Unresolved Trauma or Past Wounds

Past experiences of abuse, betrayal, or failure can create emotional scars that hinder resilience. Without healing, these wounds may become internal obstacles that inhibit perseverance. God, however, is a healer of broken hearts (Psalm 147:3). Counseling, spiritual direction, and inner healing ministries can be crucial tools for overcoming these deep obstacles and stepping into spiritual wholeness.

Recognizing these barriers is not an admission of defeat—it is a courageous step toward victory. Through honest reflection, supportive community, and spiritual discipline, believers can confront and dismantle the forces that hinder their growth in perseverance. The journey of resilience is not about never stumbling; it is about rising again, fortified by grace and anchored in hope.

Conclusion: The Journey of Perseverance

Resilience is not merely about withstanding pressure but being spiritually formed through it. The journey of perseverance in the Christian life is a testament to God's sanctifying power in His people. Trials are not anomalies—they are tools. They chisel away what is superficial, strengthen what is eternal, and anchor the soul in divine truth. As Paul wrote in Romans 8:37, "In all these things we are more than conquerors through him who loved us."

This chapter has illuminated how resilience is woven through theology, biblical witness, historical endurance, spiritual disciplines, and personal transformation. It has also shown that obstacles, though formidable, are not final. The believer's hope rests in a Savior who endured the cross and triumphed over it, inviting His followers to partake in that same overcoming spirit.

Let this not be a mere intellectual exercise. True resilience is forged in practice—in daily surrender, tested faith, and reliance on the Holy Spirit. As believers continue this spiritual journey, may they grow in strength, rooted deeply in God's promises, and resolved to run with endurance the race marked out for them (Heb. 12:1–2). In doing so, they reflect the perseverance of Christ Himself, the ultimate example and enabler of resilient faith.

Endurance, then, is not optional—it is essential. Moreover, those who endure, Scripture promises, will be crowned not just with heavenly reward, but with the joy of having lived faithfully and fully for the glory of God.

The Dwelling Place

Chapter 8

Walk in Spiritual Authority — Embracing Identity, Power, and Responsibility in Christ

Spiritual authority is the gracious endowment of power and responsibility that God gives His people so they can partner with Him in advancing His purposes on earth. Whereas Chapter 7 explored resilience as the internal fortitude required to persevere, this chapter considers authority as the external empowerment that flows from union with Christ. When believers grasp who they are *in* Christ and live *from* that identity, they can pray boldly, serve confidently, and confront darkness with holy courage. However, authority is never a license for domination; it is a sacred trust to be stewarded in humility and obedience.

This chapter will (1) trace the theological foundations of spiritual authority, (2) survey biblical paradigms of delegated power, (3) glean historical insights from Spirit-empowered movements, (4) outline practical disciplines for walking in authority, (5) expose common distortions and obstacles, and (6) offer a pastoral conclusion that anchors authority in Christlike character.

Theological Foundations of Authority

Christian authority is **rooted in the Triune life of God** and **expressed through covenant, kingdom, and new-creation identity**. Scripture depicts authority as a sacred partnership in which God delegates His rule to humankind for the flourishing of creation and the advance of redemption.

At its core, biblical authority rests on three inter-locking pillars:

1. **Creation Mandate** — Humanity is commissioned to "fill the earth and subdue it; rule over... every living creature" (Gen 1:28). This *imago Dei* vocation establishes representational authority as a creational gift.[75]

2. **Christ's Exaltation** — After His resurrection, Jesus declared, "All authority in heaven and on earth has been given to Me. Therefore go..." (Matt 28:18-19). Delegated power for mission flows from the enthroned Christ.[76]

3. **Spirit Empowerment** — At Pentecost, the risen Lord "poured out" the Spirit, clothing believers with "power from on high" (Acts 1:8; 2:33). Charisms are present-tense expressions of the Messiah's reign.[77]

---

[75] G. K. Beale, The Temple and the Church's Mission (Downers Grove, IL: IVP Academic, 2004).

[76] N. T. Wright, Matthew for Everyone, Part 2 (Louisville, KY: Westminster John Knox, 2004).

[77] Craig S. Keener, Acts: An Exegetical Commentary, vol. 1 (Grand Rapids, MI: Baker Academic, 2012).

1.1 Covenant and Kingdom

In the Ancient Near-Eastern world, covenants conferred **status** and **agency** upon royal vassals. Likewise, the biblical covenants (Noahic, Abrahamic, Mosaic, Davidic, New) progressively reveal Yahweh's desire to share governance with His people.[78] George Eldon Ladd argues that Jesus' proclamation of the Kingdom reasserts the Genesis mandate under a new covenant head, inviting believers to share in His royal dominion.[79] Thus, authority is not an add-on for the spiritually elite; it is covenantal identity for every member of God's household.

1.2 Adoption and Union with Christ

Paul grounds spiritual authority in **adoption** (*huiothesia*) and **union with Christ**. Believers are "seated with Him in the heavenly realms" (Eph 2:6), signaling a positional authority that transcends earthly structures. Ridderbos notes that being "in Christ" locates the Church within the exalted Messiah's cosmic reign, making authority *corporate* before it is *individual*.[80] Authority is therefore exercised from a place of rest, not striving.

1.3 Priestly-Kingly Vocation

Peter calls the Church "a royal priesthood" (1 Pet 2:9). This two-fold vocation synthesizes **representation**

---

[78] Sandra L. Richter, The Epic of Eden (Downers Grove, IL: IVP Academic, 2008).
[79] George Eldon Ladd, A Theology of the New Testament (Grand Rapids, MI: Eerdmans, 1993).
[80] Herman Ridderbos, Paul: An Outline of His Theology (Grand Rapids, MI: Eerdmans, 1975).

(priest) and **governance (king)**. Michael Heiser observes that priest-kings mediate God's presence outward while administering His justice inward.[81] Healthy authority always holds worship and governance in tension—prayer fuels power; holiness anchors influence.

1.4 Eschatological Tension

Spiritual authority operates in the "already/not-yet." Believers taste the powers of the age to come (Heb 6:5) yet groan under present weakness (Rom 8:23). Tom Schreiner warns that over-realized eschatology breeds triumphalism, whereas under-realized eschatology produces passivity.[82] Balanced authority acknowledges present empowerment while anticipating consummation.

1.5 Missional Orientation

Finally, authority is **missional**. Jesus bestows power *so* His disciples can "make disciples of all nations" (Matt 28:18-20). Dallas Willard writes, "The aim of God in history is the creation of an all-inclusive community of loving persons with Himself at the center… and that is what spiritual authority exists to serve."[83] Authority divorced from mission calcifies into self-promotion.

---

[81] Michael S. Heiser, The Unseen Realm (Bellingham, WA: Lexham Press, 2015).

[82] Thomas R. Schreiner, Paul: Apostle of God's Glory in Christ (Downers Grove, IL: IVP Academic, 2001).

[83] Dallas Willard, The Spirit of the Disciplines (San Francisco: Harper & Row, 1988).

Summary: Christian authority is covenantal in origin, christological in center, pneumatological in power, priestly-and kingly in vocation, eschatological in tension, and missional in purpose. Any theology or practice of authority that neglects these contours risks distortion.

2 Biblical Paradigms of Delegated Power

The sweep of Scripture provides a multi-velvet tapestry of delegated power—from Eden to Pentecost—demonstrating *how* God entrusts authority to humans, *why* He does so, and *what* healthy authority looks like in diverse contexts. By surveying key paradigms, we can discern recurring motifs:

- Stewardship – authority is always linked to caring for something or someone beyond oneself.

- Commissioning – God's call precedes human action; the initiative is divine, not self-generated.

- Moral Alignment – legitimate power is tethered to covenant faithfulness and holiness.

- Missional Purpose – authority is granted for God's redemptive agenda, never for personal glory.

The following table highlights seven representative snapshots, each illustrating a fresh dimension of delegated power.

Biblical Paradigms of Delegated Power

Paradigm	Text	Key Insight
Adam & Eve	Gen 1–2	Authority is tethered to stewardship of creation.
Moses	Exod 3–4	Divine commissioning overcomes personal inadequacy.
Davidic Kingship	2 Sam 7	Legitimate royal authority is covenantal and servant-oriented.
Prophetic Office	Jer 1:4-10	Prophets wield authority to *build and plant, tear down and uproot.*
Jesus the Messiah	Mk 1:27	His word carries intrinsic authority over demons, disease, and nature.[4]
The Twelve / Seventy-Two	Lk 9–10	Authority is delegated, missional, and confirmed by 'kingdom works'.
Apostolic Church	Acts 4:33	Great power is wed to great grace and communal generosity.

These paradigms reveal that genuine authority is always missional (for others), moral (aligned with covenant holiness), and ministerial (expressed in service, not status).

3 Historical Insights

Across twenty centuries, the Church has wrestled with the gift—and peril—of spiritual power. A diachronic glance reveals five watershed eras in which faithful believers modeled (or abused) authority, leaving lessons for every generation.

132

The Patristic Martyrs (2nd–4th centuries). During waves of Roman persecution, bishops such as Ignatius of Antioch and Polycarp of Smyrna exercised *moral* rather than *military* power. Ignatius exhorted churches to unity around their overseers because doctrinal fidelity safeguarded freedom; yet when hauled to Rome, he embraced martyrdom, declaring, "Permit me to be an imitator of the passion of my God."[84] Polycarp's calm refusal to blaspheme Christ before the pro-consul illustrated authority rooted in witness rather than coercion. Their blood became seed, proving that the Church's most significant influence flows from sacrificial love.

Celtic Mission and Monastic Authority (5th–7th centuries). In a fractured post-Roman Europe, itinerant monk-evangelists like Patrick, Columba, and Aidan established communities that blended contemplative prayer with daring evangelism. Bede records that Columba's reputation for holiness granted him persuasive authority among Pictish chieftains; miracles and hospitality opened doors where political leverage could not.[85] Celtic abbots governed through *anam chara* (soul-friend) mentorship, illustrating relational rather than hierarchical leadership.

The Magisterial Reformers (16th century). Martin Luther's defiance at Worms ("My conscience is captive to the Word of God") reanchored authority in Scripture, challenging both papal decrees and popular tradition.[86] John Calvin extended this

---

[84] Ignatius of Antioch, The Epistles of Ignatius, in Early Christian Writings, trans. Andrew Louth (London: Penguin, 1987), 107–110

[85] Bede, Ecclesiastical History of the English People, trans. Leo Sherley Price (London: Penguin Classics, 1990), 172–176.

[86] Martin Luther, The Freedom of a Christian, trans. Mark Tranvik (Minneapolis, MN: Fortress Press, 2008), 50–52

principle, teaching that the Spirit's inward witness authenticates Scripture's outward authority—thus Word and Spirit form a double helix of legitimate power.[87] Yet the violent aftermath of the Reformation also warns that truth welded to the sword of the state can mutate into oppression.

The Wesleyan-Methodist Revivals (18th century). John Wesley re-framed authority as *expedient for mission*: field preaching, class meetings, and lay exhorters broke conventional molds to reach the poor. Wesley insisted that *holiness of heart and life* undergirds charismatic authority, famously writing, "God cannot long bless a work that is not pure."[88] His disciplined societies balanced fervor with accountability, demonstrating that structure can protect—not quench—spiritual fire.

Pentecostal and Charismatic Renewal (20th–21st centuries). From Azusa Street (1906) to the Global South explosion, Pentecostals reclaimed Acts-style power for evangelism, healing, and social uplift. Historian Allan Anderson notes that pneumatological authority democratized ministry: women, the poor, and ethnic minorities preached, planted churches, and confronted injustice.[89] Yet scandals within some mega-ministries also expose the danger of gifting outrunning character, reminding modern leaders that anointing must be yoked to accountability.

---

[87] John Calvin, Institutes of the Christian Religion, ed. John T. McNeill, trans. Ford Lewis Battles (Philadelphia: Westminster Press, 1960), 1.7.4
[88] John Wesley, The Works of John Wesley (Grand Rapids, MI: Baker, 1986), 13:258.
[89] Allan Anderson, An Introduction to Pentecostalism: Global Charismatic Christianity (Cambridge: Cambridge University Press, 2013), 45–60

Taken together, these epochs teach that spiritual authority flourishes where (1) the Word governs conscience, (2) the Spirit empowers mission, and (3) Character constrains charisma. Whenever one element eclipses the others, authority corrodes into authoritarianism or impotence. Therefore, the Church of the twenty-first century must hold Scripture, Spirit, and Sanctity in creative tension—leading with cruciform humility while exercising resurrection power.

4 Practical Disciplines for Walking in Authority

Spiritual authority matures through deliberate practice. Five interconnected disciplines help believers internalize their royal–priestly identity and minister from a place of humble confidence.

Identity Immersion. First, we must habitually immerse our minds in the truths of Ephesians 1–2, Romans 8, and other "in-Christ" passages. Meditation, confession, and sung worship re-script the heart, replacing orphan mind-sets with sonship. As believers rehearse that they are seated with Christ in the heavenly realms, shame and inferiority lose their grip, making space for Spirit-breathed boldness. Identity work is not narcissistic introspection; it is agreeing with what God already declares to be true.

Obedience and Holiness. Moral authority undergirds ministerial authority. Paul likens the useful servant to "a vessel for noble purposes, cleansed and set apart" (2 Tim 2:21). Daily, ordinary choices—financial integrity, sexual purity, truthful speech—reinforce or erode the platform from which Kingdom power flows. Obedience may appear mundane, yet it is the crucible in which trustworthiness is proven.

Word-Saturated Prayer. Authority is exercised most fruitfully when Scripture shapes intercession. Praying the Psalms, apostolic prayers (e.g., Eph 1:17-23), and Jesus' own petitions align our requests with heaven's decrees. This practice forms a double-edge: the Word renews the mind while the Spirit ignites the heart, producing petitions that resonate with divine intent rather than personal ambition.

Spirit-Led Risk. Authority grows by use. Like the servants in Jesus' parable of the minas, believers discover increase only when they trade with what they have been given. Spirit-prompted risks—offering to pray for the sick, sharing Christ at work, confronting injustice—stretch faith-muscles and confirm that the same power that raised Jesus from the dead is active in us today (Acts 14:3). Without risk, authority atrophies into theory.

Accountable Community. Finally, healthy authority is never isolated. Acts 13 portrays prophets and teachers discerning the Spirit together before commissioning Paul and Barnabas. In a covenant community, our gifts are tested, motives purified, and blind spots exposed—mutual submission guards against authoritarian drift and anchors charisma in the safety of shared discernment.

Practised in concert, these disciplines transform raw positional authority into mature, reliable power fit for Kingdom service. They cultivate a leader whose voice carries weight not because of title but because heaven recognizes a life yielded to the King.

Obstacles and Distortions

Even with a biblically balanced theology of authority, believers encounter formidable barriers that can dilute or distort their influence. Four obstacles are prevalent:

Fear and Inferiority. Like Jeremiah—who protested that he was "only a youth" (Jer 1:6)—many Christians shrink from spiritual responsibility, convinced they are unqualified. This inner timidity muzzles prayer, muffles proclamation, and keeps gifts buried. The antidote is a steady diet of identity-immersion: remembering that God not only calls but also equips, touching Jeremiah's mouth and promising His presence (Jer 1:7-9). Confidence grows when we fix our eyes more on the Sender than on our inadequacy.

Pride and Control. At the opposite extreme, authority can intoxicate. Diotrephes, who "loves to be first" (3 Jn 9), illustrates how ego distorts leadership into domination. When influence becomes a quest for status, the fruit is manipulation, exclusion, and spiritual coercion. Humility—expressed through mutual submission and willingness to be corrected—is the safeguard. Leaders who routinely surrender agenda, platform, and reputation back to Christ keep ambition on the altar and authority in healthy channels.

Theological Cessationism. Paul warns of those who exhibit "a form of godliness but deny its power" (2 Tim 3:5). When believers adopt a worldview that confines the Spirit's gifts to the first century, they unwittingly amputate dimensions of their inheritance. Such skepticism breeds prayerlessness and a church culture of low-expectation. The remedy is a fresh encounter with

Scripture's testimony and the Spirit's present work—allowing experience to be shaped by the Word, not the other way around.

Wounds from Spiritual Abuse. Some saints recoil from authority because they have tasted its misuse—controlling leadership, prophetic manipulation, or legalistic shame. Trauma produces suspicion; submitting feels dangerous. Healing begins with lament and honest storytelling in a safe community, followed by exposure to servant-hearted mentors who embody the gentleness of Christ. Redeemed authority does not erase wounds but transforms them into testimonies of restoration.

Recognizing these hindrances enables believers to seek targeted grace—boldness for fear, humility for pride, expectancy for skepticism, and healing for hurt—so that authority is exercised in purity and power.

Conclusion

Spiritual authority is a sacred trust that flows from identity (who we are in Christ), intimacy (walking with the Spirit), and integrity (living in holiness and humility). Throughout this chapter, we have traced its theological roots— from the Creation Mandate to Pentecostal empowerment— observed its biblical and historical exemplars, and laid out disciplines that keep authority aligned with heaven's purposes.

When God's people internalize their adoption, saturate their prayers with the Word, take Spirit-led risks, and remain anchored in accountable community, their influence becomes both weighty and winsome—weighty because it carries heaven's endorsement, winsome because it manifests Christ's gentleness. Conversely, where fear, pride, skepticism, or past abuse dominate, authority is suppressed or warped, diminishing the Church's witness.

Our era is marked by unprecedented turmoil and opportunity. Creation groans, cultures fragment, and yet the gospel surges forward. Christ is still issuing His Great Commission based on *all* authority in heaven and earth. Therefore, let every reader hear the summons: receive the royal-priestly mantle, cultivate character equal to power, and steward authority as Jesus did—washing feet, healing wounds, proclaiming liberty. Then the world will glimpse the in-breaking reign of the crucified and risen King through a humble yet authoritative Church.

--- Spiritual authority is a sacred trust flowing from union with the exalted Christ and empowered by the Holy Spirit. It is exercised in humility, stewarded in community, authenticated by holiness, and directed toward mission. When believers walk in this balanced authority, they become conduits of God's Kingdom—healing the broken, liberating the oppressed, and proclaiming the reign of Christ until He comes.

The Dwelling Place

Chapter 9

Build Life-Giving Relationships — Cultivating Christlike Community

Relationships are the lifeblood of the Christian life. From the Triune fellowship of the Godhead to the communion of saints, Scripture portrays life in God as inherently relational. The gospel reconciles individuals to God and restores relationships among people. In an age marked by individualism, isolation, and digital disconnection, building life-giving relationships is both a prophetic witness and a practical necessity for believers seeking to mirror the communal love of the Trinity.

This chapter explores the depth and beauty of cultivating a Christlike community, emphasizing how the relational nature of God forms the foundation for all meaningful connections. We will delve into Jesus' model of ministry that prioritized intimacy and transformation, examine the powerful "one-another" commands that define Kingdom culture, and uncover the cultural and spiritual barriers that obstruct authentic relationships. From there, we will discover transformative practices that can help believers create environments where grace flourishes and community thrives.

By tracing biblical and practical pathways to relational maturity, this chapter equips readers to foster Christ-centered community in every sphere of life—from church gatherings and small groups to families and friendships. We aim to provide theological insights and actionable steps to become conduits of God's love in an increasingly fragmented world. In doing so, we reflect the heart of Christ and participate in His redemptive work of reconciling people to Himself and to one another.. From the Triune fellowship of the Godhead to the communion of saints, Scripture portrays life in God as inherently relational. The gospel reconciles individuals to God and restores relationships among people. In an age marked by individualism, isolation, and digital disconnection, building life-giving relationships is both a prophetic witness and a practical necessity for believers seeking to mirror the communal love of the Trinity.

This chapter unpacks what it means to cultivate a Christlike community by exploring: (1) the relational nature of God, (2) Jesus' communal ministry model, (3) the one-another commands that shape New Testament relationships, (4) the barriers to authentic connection, (5) the practices that foster transformative relationships, and (6) a concluding exhortation to embody Kingdom community. The goal is to equip the reader with theological understanding and practical tools to become a conduit of God's love in every relational context.

1. The Relational Nature of God

God is not a solitary being. At the heart of Christian theology is the mystery of the Trinity—one God in three persons: Father, Son, and Holy Spirit. This eternal communion reveals that love is not something God does, but who God is (1 John 4:8). The divine life is marked by mutual indwelling, joy, and shared purpose. Relationship is God's nature and central to God's work in the world.

The Trinity reveals a God who has never existed in isolation. From eternity past, the Father has loved the Son in the Spirit, forming a divine communion that is perfect, self-sufficient, and gloriously relational. This love spills outward into creation—not out of need, but out of the abundance of divine joy. Creation itself is an overflow of divine love, inviting humanity into the relational dance of the Godhead.

According to theologian Michael Reeves, "The Father, Son, and Spirit are so united in love that God is the eternally outgoing and others-centered God."[90] This internal fellowship sets the pattern for all human relationships. Created in God's image (Gen 1:27), humanity was designed for communion with God and community with one another. We are not merely rational or moral beings—we are relational beings because we reflect a relational God.

Being made in God's image also means relational wholeness, which is integral to our discipleship. Sin fractures the connection—not only with God, but with each other. The fall introduced alienation, suspicion, and shame, replacing the intimacy of Eden with isolation. Redemption is not merely personal salvation but the restoration of God's image through renewed relationships. The gospel heals our vertical relationship with God and our horizontal relationships with others, forging a new humanity united by grace (Eph 2:14–16).

Moreover, this relational aspect of God's nature defines the Church's mission. We are not saved into isolation, but into a family. The Church becomes the living embodiment of God's

---

[90] Reeves, Michael. *Delighting in the Trinity*. Downers Grove, IL: InterVarsity Press, 2012

relational character—a place where love is practiced, hospitality is extended, and burdens are shared. As we embrace God's relational essence, we discover our deepest purpose: to love God fully and love others well, fostering a community that reflects the divine harmony of heaven on earth.

Every meaningful human relationship is an echo of the divine communion. Whether in marriage, friendship, mentorship, or church fellowship, we are called to mirror the Trinity by living in joyful, sacrificial love. In doing so, we become a prophetic witness to a fragmented world—a testimony that relational restoration is not only possible but eternal, rooted in the very being of God.

2. Jesus' Model of Relational Ministry

Jesus' earthly ministry was profoundly relational. He did not operate from a distance or rely solely on public proclamations; instead, He embedded Himself in the rhythms of everyday life, forming intentional relationships with a diverse group of people. His life demonstrates that discipleship is not a program but a relational journey marked by presence, patience, and love.

Jesus called twelve disciples to walk with Him—not merely to receive instruction but to experience life together. He ate with them, traveled with them, corrected them, and empowered them. He modeled what it means to live in community: to forgive seventy times seven, to serve without recognition, and to share in both sorrow and celebration. His inner circle, including Peter, James, and John, reveals that even within the broader context of community, deeper layers of relational intimacy were nurtured.

He crossed social, ethnic, and moral boundaries to extend relationship and grace. Whether dining with tax collectors, healing lepers, or conversing with a Samaritan woman at a well, Jesus consistently prioritized people over social norms and religious expectations. His relationships were not transactional—they were transformational. He saw people in their brokenness and responded with compassion that restored dignity and belonging.

Furthermore, Jesus' approach to spiritual formation was rooted in relational environments. Yes, he taught the crowds, but invested most deeply in a few. His model was incarnational—He was "God with us" (Matt. 1:23), showing that proximity matters. Transformation often happens in shared life, where love is tested and grace is given.

The relational rhythm of Jesus' ministry also included rest and solitude. He withdrew to desolate places to commune with the Father, demonstrating that healthy relationships with others stem from a vibrant relationship with God. His example teaches that sustainable ministry requires inner replenishment, lest relationships become strained by unhealed wounds or exhausted hearts.

Ultimately, Jesus' ministry culminated in the Cross—the greatest relational act of love in history. In giving His life, He reconciled humanity to the Father and one another, tearing down the dividing wall of hostility (Eph. 2:14). His resurrection formed a new community, the Church, empowered by the Spirit to continue His relational mission. As His followers, we are called to extend this same self-giving love, cultivating environments where trust, empathy, and transformation abound.

3. The One-Another Commands

Practicing the "One Another" Way of Life

The New Testament contains over fifty "one another" commands that outline the relational ethics of the Kingdom of God. These are not mere suggestions for harmonious living; they are divine imperatives shaping how believers embody Christ in community. Commands such as "love one another" (John 13:34), "bear with one another" (Eph. 4:2), "forgive one another" (Col. 3:13), and "encourage one another" (1 Thess. 5:11) form the backbone of Christian relational life.

These commands emerge from the reality of the early Church, which faced cultural, linguistic, and economic diversity. The unity of the body was not a given; it had to be cultivated. The apostles urged believers to pursue peace, patience, and mutual care proactively. The early Christians understood that embodying the gospel meant committing to one another in authentic, sacrificial love. These commands functioned as a spiritual liturgy for community life, reminding believers that faith is personal but never private.

Practicing the "one another" commands is a communal spiritual discipline that requires intentionality, humility, and grace. Each command reflects the nature of God and reveals what it means to live in authentic, Spirit-led fellowship. These are not isolated actions but a way of life—a rhythm of reciprocal love and accountability that fosters spiritual growth.

The Church becomes a relational sanctuary when believers commit to living out these commands. Instead of transactional interactions, relationships are built on covenantal love. Conflicts become opportunities for reconciliation, weaknesses invite support rather than shame, and diversity becomes a strength instead of a threat. The "one another" way cultivates environments where grace, truth, and transformation can flourish.

Embracing this vision of relational life calls for a culture shift in many churches—from individualism to interdependence, from programs to people, from hierarchy to shared life. It requires us to slow down, listen deeply, confess honestly, and serve sacrificially. In doing so, we not only obey Christ's commands—we become a visible demonstration of the gospel's power to reconcile and restore.

4. Barriers to Relational Connection in a Fragmented Age

Despite relational community's biblical and theological richness, many believers today struggle to build and maintain deep, life-giving connections. Authentic relationships often take a backseat to convenience and comfort in a culture increasingly shaped by individualism, consumerism, and digital mediation. The challenges are both external and internal, and they must be named and confronted if we hope to embody the communal ethic of the Kingdom.

One of the most pervasive obstacles is the idol of autonomy. Western culture prizes independence and self-sufficiency, often interpreting dependence or vulnerability as weakness. This worldview starkly contrasts the interdependent model of the Church described in Scripture—a body where each member needs the other (1 Cor. 12:12–27). When autonomy is idolized, community is treated as optional rather than essential, leading to relational superficiality and isolation.

Another significant barrier is busyness. Many Christians are overcommitted, running from one obligation to another with little margin for meaningful engagement. In such an environment, relationships become transactional—reduced to quick text messages or obligatory Sunday greetings. Deep community requires time, presence, and shared experiences, none of which can flourish in a life without room for connection.

Woundedness also hinders relational depth. Many carry scars from past betrayals, church hurts, or dysfunctional family dynamics. As a result, they approach relationships with guarded hearts, always expecting rejection or disappointment. Without intentional healing and discipleship, these wounds calcify into cynicism and detachment, making genuine connection unsafe or unattainable.

Technology, while offering new forms of connection, also poses challenges. Social media can foster a false sense of intimacy without requiring the vulnerability of face-to-face interaction. Algorithms reinforce echo chambers, and online personas mask real struggles. While digital tools can supplement community, they must never replace the embodied reality of living life with others in the presence of God.

Additionally, consumerism infiltrates the Church, shaping how people view relationships. Instead of approaching the community with a mindset of service and covenant, many view it through the lens of preference and performance. Churches are evaluated like products, and relationships are sustained only when they meet personal needs. This mentality undermines the biblical vision of mutual commitment and perseverance.

Overcoming these barriers requires a renewed vision of what it means to belong. It means exchanging independence for interdependence, busyness for availability, guardedness for vulnerability, and consumption for covenant. It means believing that community is not an accessory to the Christian life but its very expression. As we allow the Spirit to dismantle these barriers, we make room for the kind of relational flourishing that reflects the love of Christ and invites others into His redemptive embrace.

5. Practices for Cultivating Christlike Community

To build life-giving relationships, the following practices can help churches and individuals create spaces where community flourishes:

Shared Rhythms. Regular gatherings for meals, prayer, and Scripture foster intimacy. Acts 2:46 describes the early church as breaking bread "with glad and sincere hearts," cultivating unity and joy. Rhythms build roots and anchor us in shared life.

Hospitality. Inviting others into our homes and lives reflects God's welcome to us. Hebrews 13:2 reminds us that by showing hospitality, some have entertained angels unawares. Hospitality transforms strangers into friends and friends into family. Radical hospitality fosters belonging and breaks down walls of loneliness and suspicion.

Confession and Forgiveness. James 5:16 urges believers to "confess your sins to one another" and pray for healing. This mutual vulnerability and grace deepen trust and authenticity. Confession breaks shame; forgiveness builds bridges. When practiced consistently, these actions form the heartbeat of redemptive community.

Celebration and Mourning Together. Romans 12:15 exhorts us to "rejoice with those who rejoice; mourn with those who mourn." Shared emotional experiences bond communities in both joy and sorrow. In laughter and in lament, we meet one another deeply. Spiritual friendship is built in these holy moments.

Mutual Discipleship. Spiritual growth accelerates when believers challenge, encourage, and learn from one another. Paul told Timothy to entrust teaching to faithful men who would teach others also (2 Tim 2:2). Life-on-life discipleship builds maturity. Iron sharpens iron in the community.

Service and Sacrifice. Relationships grow through self-giving love. Serving one another in tangible ways—providing meals, helping with needs, or simply being present—demonstrates the servant heart of Christ. Community thrives when we take up the towel and basin, following Jesus' example.

Listening and Storytelling. Listening is a sacred act. When we hear one another's stories without judgment, we create space for dignity and connection. Telling our testimonies reminds us of God's faithfulness and helps others find courage in their journey. Narratives weave hearts together and build spiritual empathy.

In cultivating these practices, we witness the formation of a spiritual family where love is practiced, burdens are shared, and Christ is glorified. These are not one-time actions, but ongoing habits that shape the culture of community over time. Healthy relationships are not accidental but built on purpose with consistency, compassion, and intentional spiritual formation.

Conclusion

Life-giving relationships are not peripheral to the Christian faith but central to its expression. Rooted in the relational nature of the Triune God, modeled by Jesus, and shaped by the one-another commands, community is both a gift and a calling.

In a fragmented world, the Church is called to embody a different way of being—a Kingdom culture marked by love, hospitality, and mutual care. As believers commit to practicing relational disciplines and overcoming cultural barriers, the Church becomes a living testimony of God's reconciling power.

When Christians build life-giving relationships, they reflect the heart of Christ, draw others to the gospel, and experience the joy of being known, loved, and transformed in community. These relationships are not merely for survival—they are the environment in which faith flourishes, mission advances, and Christ is revealed through His people.

Let us press beyond surface-level interaction into authentic spiritual friendship. Let us be a people who rejoice in one another's wins, walk alongside in times of weakness, and labor together for the glory of God. In doing so, we embody heaven's harmony on earth.

Let our homes become places of refuge. Let our churches become tables of grace. Let our hearts remain open, expectant, and willing to love as Christ first loved us. In this kind of community, we reflect the gospel and live it.

The Dwelling Place

Chapter 10

Serve with Open Hands: Practicing Generosity and Compassion in Action

Serving others is at the heart of the Christian life. From the earliest moments of Jesus' public ministry to His final moments on the cross, the theme of self-giving love permeates the Gospel story. In a culture driven by consumption, self-interest, and personal advancement, Jesus presents a radically different model—greatness is found in humility, and power is expressed through sacrificial service. Serving with open hands is not simply about engaging in charitable acts; it reflects the very character of Christ and the redemptive mission of God in the world.

This chapter explores the theological and biblical foundations of service, drawing on the life and teachings of Jesus as the ultimate example of generous compassion. It examines the disciplines and postures required to cultivate a servant's heart and outlines service's transformative impact on both the giver and the receiver. We also confront the cultural and spiritual obstacles that hinder generosity and compassion, offering practical strategies for believers to embody a lifestyle of Kingdom-centered service.

When believers serve with open hands, they participate in the divine economy of grace—where resources are shared, burdens are lifted, and communities are strengthened. In this way, service becomes an act of obedience and a sacred privilege. Through consistent, Spirit-led generosity and compassion, the Church becomes a witness to a watching world, showcasing the heart of a Savior who "did not come to be served, but to serve" (Mark 10:45).

The Servant Heart of Jesus

Jesus Christ, the Son of God, came not to dominate, but to serve. Throughout the Gospels, we find Him healing the sick, feeding the hungry, washing His disciples' feet, and welcoming those society had cast aside. His ministry was not marked by comfort or convenience but by compassion and self-emptying love (Philippians 2:5–7). As theologian N.T. Wright explains, "The central thing that Jesus did during His public career was to reconstitute the people of God around Himself by acts of generous healing and welcome."[91]

The Gospel of John provides one of the most profound images of Jesus' humility and servant leadership. On the night of His betrayal, Jesus stooped to wash His disciples' feet—an act reserved for the lowliest servant (John 13:1–17). This gesture was not merely symbolic but a demonstration of the type of love He expected from His followers. Jesus framed it plainly: "Now that I, your Lord and Teacher, have washed your feet, you also should wash one another's feet" (John 13:14).

The cross itself represents the ultimate act of service. Jesus laid down His life not only as a ransom for sin but as a supreme example of love in action. The apostle Paul captures this

---

[91] Wright, N.T. *How God Became King: The Forgotten Story of the Gospels.* New York: HarperOne, 2012.

beautifully in Galatians 2:20, stating, "The Son of God...loved me and gave himself for me." Christ's death was not coerced but voluntary, driven by compassion for humanity.

By embodying this sacrificial spirit, Jesus established a new model of leadership and influence, turning cultural norms upside down. Rather than lording authority over others, He taught that the greatest in the Kingdom is the one who serves (Matthew 23:11). This redefinition of greatness invites all believers to see service not as an option, but as a calling intrinsic to their identity in Christ.

This servant-hearted orientation did not waver under pressure. Whether He was exhausted from ministry or grieving personal loss, Jesus continually made Himself available to those in need. He healed Jairus's daughter while en route to help another, multiplied loaves and fish to feed thousands, and still found time to restore Peter after his denial. This consistency in service reveals not just what Jesus did—but who He was. He served because He loved deeply and unconditionally. For believers, this is the ultimate template: to serve as a natural outflow of love rather than as an obligation. Our call is to do what Jesus did and become as He is—marked by compassion, fueled by humility, and anchored in divine love.

Biblical Foundations of Service

The biblical mandate for service is woven throughout the Old and New Testaments, establishing it as a core expression of faithful discipleship and covenantal living. From the Mosaic Law to the teachings of Jesus and the epistles of Paul, service is not a peripheral duty—it is central to God's redemptive plan for humanity.

In the Old Testament, service was integral to the identity of God's people. The Israelites were repeatedly reminded to care for the poor, the stranger, and the marginalized, because they themselves had once been enslaved people in Egypt (Deut. 15:11; Lev. 19:34). The prophets regularly called out Israel's failure to uphold justice and mercy, emphasizing that true worship included acts of service and compassion (Isaiah 58:6–10; Micah 6:8).

Jesus amplified this call in His earthly ministry. He taught that serving others is synonymous with serving God Himself. In the parable of the sheep and the goats, Jesus identified Himself with the hungry, the stranger, the sick, and the imprisoned: "Whatever you did for one of the least of these brothers and sisters of mine, you did for me" (Matthew 25:40). This profound identification reveals that service to others is sacred—it is service rendered unto Christ.

The early church embodied this ethic of service in its communal life. Acts 2:42–47 describes a community marked by mutual care, generosity, and sacrificial sharing. The apostles taught that spiritual gifts were given not for personal status but for the building up of the body of Christ (1 Cor. 12:7). Paul exhorted believers to "serve one another humbly in love" (Galatians 5:13) and to "carry each other's burdens" (Galatians 6:2).

Even more, service in Scripture is not restricted to certain roles or functions; it is the shared calling of every believer. Peter affirms this in 1 Peter 4:10: "Each of you should use whatever gift you have received to serve others, as faithful stewards of God's grace." Service, then, becomes the tangible outworking of love—the kind of love that imitates Christ and manifests the Kingdom of God on earth.

The scale of the act does not measure biblical service, but by the spirit in which it is offered. Whether offering a cup of cold water or laying down one's life, every act done in Jesus' name becomes a seed of the Kingdom. In this way, the biblical call to serve with open hands is both a commission and a privilege, a sacred invitation to partner with God in the renewal of all things.

Cultivating a Generous Spirit

Cultivating a generous spirit begins with a transformation of the heart and mind. It is rooted in an awareness that all we have belongs to God and is meant to be stewarded for His glory. Generosity is not confined to material possessions; it encompasses time, talent, energy, attention, and compassion. The generous person lives with open hands and an open heart, ready to respond to the needs of others with grace and intentionality.

This kind of generosity flows from gratitude. When we recognize the depth of God's provision and love in our lives, we are moved to reflect that love through acts of kindness and giving. Generosity becomes a natural response to grace, rather than an obligation. It is not transactional—it is relational, modeled after the lavish generosity of God, who "did not spare his own Son, but gave him up for us all" (Romans 8:32).

Furthermore, generosity must be cultivated through spiritual discipline. Just as one trains the body for strength, the heart must be trained to give freely and joyfully. This may involve reorienting our values, developing new giving habits, and practicing intentional acts of service in our communities. Giving regularly—even in small ways—develops a lifestyle of abundance rather than scarcity, reminding us that God is our source.

A generous spirit also requires trust. Letting go can feel risky in a culture driven by accumulation and self-preservation. However, faith reminds us that we are not our providers—God is. We can give freely because we serve a God who gives abundantly. As we lean into this trust, generosity becomes a reflection of our faith, a tangible expression of our belief that God's Kingdom is one of provision, sufficiency, and grace.

Finally, cultivating a generous spirit reshapes our relationships. It breaks down walls of selfishness and pride and fosters connection, empathy, and shared humanity. When we serve others with generosity, we affirm their worth, uplift their dignity, and echo the heart of Christ. In this way, generosity is not just an act—it is a way of being, a daily practice that forms us more deeply into the image of the One who gave all.

Overcoming Barriers to Service

Despite the clear biblical call to serve with generosity and compassion, believers often encounter numerous obstacles that hinder them from fully embracing a service lifestyle. These internal and external barriers can range from personal insecurities to cultural pressures and spiritual immaturity. Understanding and addressing these obstacles is crucial for cultivating a consistent and fruitful practice of serving with open hands.

One of the most common internal barriers is the fear of inadequacy. Many believers struggle with the belief that they are not qualified, gifted, or knowledgeable enough to serve effectively. This mindset often leads to inaction, fueled by comparing with others or misunderstanding what accurate service entails. However, Scripture reminds us that God uses the weak to confound the strong (1 Corinthians 1:27), and that the willingness to serve often outweighs the perfection of the act itself. Overcoming this fear begins with trusting that God equips those He calls and that small, faithful acts can have profound Kingdom impact.

Another significant barrier is busyness. Carving out time to serve others can feel like an added burden in a fast-paced culture that prizes productivity and achievement. When schedules are overloaded and energy is depleted, serving becomes one more thing to check off a to-do list rather than a joyful response to God's love. To counter this, believers must intentionally prioritize service as an act of worship and discipleship, embedding it into the rhythms of everyday life. This may involve simplifying one's commitments, setting aside regular time for community involvement, or integrating service into family routines.

Materialism and the fear of lack can also inhibit generosity. The world often tells us that we never have enough— enough money, time, resources, or energy. This scarcity mindset can lead to hoarding rather than sharing, protectionism rather than compassion. However, the Gospel invites us into an economy of grace, where provision is abundant and trust in God's sufficiency frees us to give freely. Generosity is not about how much we have, but how willing we are to share what we have.

Additionally, spiritual apathy or immaturity can dull a believer's sensitivity to the needs of others. When one's relationship with God becomes stagnant or inward-focused, the drive to serve may wane. Reviving this sense of mission requires renewed engagement with Scripture, prayer, and community life—contexts in which the Spirit reawakens compassion and realigns the heart with God's purposes.

Finally, cultural norms can subtly discourage service. Western culture often elevates individualism, comfort, and self-fulfillment over communal responsibility and sacrifice. This worldview contradicts the call of Christ, who modeled self-emptying love and called His followers to do the same. Resisting these cultural influences demands a countercultural mindset that embraces service not as weakness but as strength, not as loss but as gain.

Overcoming these barriers begins with a posture of humility and a willingness to be transformed. As believers confront and dismantle these internal and external challenges, they grow in spiritual maturity and are empowered to serve more faithfully. In this way, the journey of serving with open hands becomes both a personal formation and a public witness—declaring to the world that the love of Christ is active, generous, and unstoppable.

The Impact of Open-Handed Living

Open-handed giving is more than a transactional act; it is a transformative spiritual practice reshaping hearts, communities, and even systems. At its core, open-handed giving reflects the generosity of God, who gave His Son for the world and continues to pour out blessings abundantly. When believers give from a posture of trust and selflessness, they embody the Gospel in motion, demonstrating to others that God's love is not hoarded but shared.

This kind of generosity breaks cycles of selfishness and scarcity. It teaches the heart to release rather than cling, to sow rather than store. By living with open hands, Christians learn to view their resources not as possessions to guard but as tools for mission. They become stewards of grace, aligning their finances, time, and energy with the purposes of God. Such giving builds resilience in the giver, deepening trust in God's provision and loosening the grip of materialism.

The impact is not limited to personal transformation. Communities are strengthened when generosity flows freely. Needs are met, burdens are lifted, and relationships are forged through acts of giving. The early church in Acts 2 models this vividly—sharing possessions so that "there were no needy persons among them." Open-handed giving thus creates an atmosphere of unity, empathy, and mutual care that reflects the Kingdom of God.

Furthermore, the testimony of generous living often opens doors for evangelism. Generosity is a compelling witness in a world marked by self-interest and division. It asks nothing in return, carries no agenda but love, and draws attention to the Source from which all blessings flow. This is why Jesus taught, "Let your light shine before others, that they may see your good deeds and glorify your Father in heaven" (Matthew 5:16).

In practicing open-handed giving, believers participate in God's ongoing renewal work. They become channels of blessing, vessels of compassion, and signs of hope in a world that desperately needs all three. The impact, then, is exponential— not just in what is given, but in what is changed because it was given. A heart unlocked by generosity can alter a life, a community, and even a culture.

Conclusion

Serving with open hands is not merely an occasional gesture of goodwill—it is a defining characteristic of a life shaped by the Gospel. Rooted in the servant heart of Jesus, empowered by biblical truth, and cultivated through intentional practice, this service lifestyle transforms those who receive and give. We become conduits of God's grace in a world desperate for hope and healing by confronting and overcoming the barriers that hinder our generosity and compassion.

The call to serve is not limited to a select few with special talents or resources. Every believer's shared mission is to have a daily opportunity to reflect Christ's love in tangible ways. Whether through small acts of kindness or significant sacrifices, our service becomes a testimony to the transforming power of the Kingdom of God. Let us, then, serve with open hands—freely, joyfully, and faithfully—knowing that in doing so, we partner with God in the renewal of all things.

Chapter 11

The Sacred Trust of Stewardship: Living with Purpose and Simplicity

In an age where accumulation and excess are often celebrated as signs of success, the biblical call to stewardship offers a radically countercultural path marked by simplicity, intentionality, and Kingdom-focused living. Stewardship, as framed in Scripture, is not merely about the prudent management of finances; it encompasses every dimension of our lives—time, talents, resources, relationships, and even the gospel itself. Living with purpose and simplicity means aligning our priorities with God's eternal values, embracing contentment, and faithfully managing what we have been entrusted with for His glory. Jesus articulated this principle plainly when He said, "From everyone who has been given much, much will be demanded" (Luke 12:48, NIV).

The believer is not the owner but a steward—called to manage the Master's resources with care and discernment. This chapter explores what it means to steward our lives with a Kingdom mindset, engaging biblical truths, theological insights, historical models, and practical steps for cultivating a lifestyle of simplicity and intentionality.

Rethinking Ownership: The Theology of Divine Entrustment

A fundamental theological truth lies at the core of biblical stewardship: God is the Creator and ultimate Owner of all things. Psalm 24:1 declares, "The earth is the Lord's, and everything in it, the world, and all who live in it." This central doctrine shapes a Christian's worldview. Our possessions, time, and lives are not ours; they belong to God. Thus, stewardship begins with recognizing that everything we have has been entrusted to us—not earned, not deserved, but graciously given.[92]

From the very beginning, humanity was commissioned to care for creation as image-bearers of God. Genesis 1:28 reveals God's original mandate—"Be fruitful and increase in number; fill the earth and subdue it. Rule over...every living creature." This was not a license for exploitation, but a sacred entrustment to reflect God's character through responsible dominion. In essence, human beings were called to be vice-regents of creation, exercising authority under the ultimate sovereignty of God.

Theologically, stewardship affirms both the transcendence and immanence of God. He is not only the Owner of all, but also intimately involved in sustaining what He has made. Acts 17:25 says that God "is not served by human hands, as if he needed anything. Rather, he himself gives everyone life and breath and everything else." Paul further exhorts believers not to place their hope in uncertain riches but in "God, who richly provides us with everything for our enjoyment" (1 Tim. 6:17).

---

[92] Randy Alcorn, Managing God's Money: A Biblical Guide (Carol Stream, IL: Tyndale, 2005).

This view of God's provision transforms stewardship from a burdensome duty into an act of worship and trust.[93]

Moreover, stewardship is teleological—it is directed toward a divine purpose. Jesus' parable of the talents (Matt. 25:14–30) illustrates that God expects fruitfulness, not complacency. The faithful stewards who multiplied their master's investment were praised and rewarded, while the one who buried his talent out of fear was rebuked. The implication is clear: God desires faithful engagement and wise management of His gifts. As Jesus taught, bearing fruit for God's Kingdom brings Him glory and affirms our discipleship (John 15:8).

This divine entrustment also requires accountability. Scripture teaches that each person will give an account for how they managed what was entrusted to them (Rom. 14:12). This accountability is not merely for financial resources. However, for every opportunity, relationship, gift, and moment we are given. Therefore, rethinking ownership leads to a life of reverent responsibility and intentional living, grounded in the understanding that we are temporary stewards of eternal treasures.[94]

Redeeming Time: Stewarding the Hours for Eternal Impact

Time is one of the most precious yet fleeting resources entrusted to humanity. Unlike material possessions that can be replenished, time, once spent, cannot be recovered. The call to steward time wisely is not simply a matter of productivity or

---

[93] Timothy Keller, Every Good Endeavor: Connecting Your Work to God's Work (New York: Dutton, 2012)

[94] George Barna, The State of the Church 2018 (Ventura, CA: Barna Group, 2018).

efficiency, but a profoundly spiritual mandate to align with God's purposes. Scripture exhorts believers to "redeem the time, because the days are evil" (Eph. 5:16, NKJV), highlighting the urgency of purposeful living in a fallen world.

Redeeming time begins with a sober awareness of its brevity. Psalm 90:12 pleads, "Teach us to number our days, that we may gain a heart of wisdom." This verse emphasizes counting days and encourages intentional living with an eternal perspective. When believers understand that their days are finite and divinely appointed, they are moved to prioritize what matters most—loving God, serving others, and advancing His Kingdom. [95]

Stewarding time well involves recognizing divine interruptions as opportunities for ministry. Jesus exemplified this throughout His earthly life. Though often surrounded by crowds and pressed for time, He was never hurried or dismissive. He stopped for the woman with the issue of blood, dined with sinners, and paused to bless children. In each instance, He demonstrated that time invested in people was never wasted. Similarly, believers are called to live with margin—creating space in their schedules to respond to the Holy Spirit's leading and others' needs.

Living with a Kingdom mindset means distinguishing between the urgent and the important. Modern life often bombards us with countless demands that can eclipse what truly matters. The discipline of Sabbath, for instance, is God's antidote to a culture of overwork and haste. It reorients our souls,

---

[95] Donald S. Whitney, Spiritual Disciplines for the Christian Life (Colorado Springs: NavPress, 2014).

reminding us that our value is not in what we produce but in who we are as beloved children of God. Regular rest, reflection, and renewal rhythms help us steward our time for tasks and transformation.[96]

Furthermore, the stewardship of time involves strategic planning and Spirit-led prioritization. Setting aside dedicated moments for prayer, Scripture meditation, discipleship, and service fosters spiritual growth and aligns daily living with eternal significance. Believers are not merely called to be busy but to be fruitful. As Jesus taught in John 15, those who abide in Him will bear much fruit. This fruitfulness is not accidental; it flows from intentional time spent in His presence and obedience to His voice.

Ultimately, redeeming time is about embracing each moment as a sacred trust. Whether in work or rest, solitude or community, routine or spontaneity, every hour is an opportunity to reflect the heart of God and partner with Him in His redemptive work. To steward time well is to live with purpose, urgency, and peace—knowing that every day lived for Christ carries eternal weight.[97]

Cultivating Generosity: The Overflow of a Kingdom Heart

Generosity is more than an act—it is an attitude, a posture of the heart that reflects the nature of God. Scripture consistently reveals a God who gives lavishly, whether in creation, redemption, or daily provision. John 3:16 states, "For God so

---

[96] James K. A. Smith, Desiring the Kingdom: Worship, Worldview, and Cultural Formation (Grand Rapids: Baker Academic, 2009).
[97] Peter Scazzero, Emotionally Healthy Discipleship (Grand Rapids: Zondervan, 2021).

loved the world that He gave..." This divine generosity is not transactional but transformational. As believers are conformed to Christ's image, they are invited into a lifestyle where giving becomes a joyful expression of love and trust.

True generosity flows from gratitude. When we recognize that all we have is a gift from God, we are moved to give freely rather than hoard fearfully. The Macedonian believers in 2 Corinthians 8 exemplify this spirit. Though in "extreme poverty," they gave with "overflowing joy" and "rich generosity" (2 Cor. 8:2, NIV). Their giving was not coerced; it was a natural outpouring of grace. Paul commends them for giving themselves first to the Lord—a reminder that generosity begins with surrender.

Living generously also requires a renewed mind that resists the pull of consumerism. In a culture obsessed with acquisition and status, Christians are called to contentment and simplicity. Hebrews 13:5 urges, "Keep your lives free from the love of money and be content with what you have." Generosity is a powerful declaration that our security and identity are rooted not in possessions but in the Provider.

Moreover, generosity extends beyond finances. It includes the giving of time, encouragement, hospitality, and presence. Jesus praised the widow who gave two small coins not because of the amount, but because of the heart behind the gift (Mark 12:41–44). In the Kingdom economy, faithfulness outweighs volume.

Practicing generosity requires intentionality. Creating a budget that prioritizes tithing, supporting missions, or helping people in need reflects a life aimed at eternal investment. Hosting others, volunteering time, and sharing talents are all ways to embody the generous heart of God. Paul reminded the Ephesian elders, "It is more blessed to give than to receive" (Acts 20:35).

Ultimately, generosity is contagious. When one life reflects the generosity of God, it inspires others to do the same, creating a ripple effect of Kingdom impact. To cultivate generosity is to embrace the truth that in giving, we reflect the very heart of our Father and sow seeds of transformation that outlast time itself.

Minimalism and Simplicity: Reclaiming the Beauty of Less

In a world driven by consumerism, minimalism and simplicity offer a redemptive vision for living well with less. These principles are not about deprivation or austerity, but about intentionality—focusing on what truly matters while releasing the distractions that weigh us down. Biblical simplicity invites believers to live uncluttered lives for greater spiritual clarity and Kingdom impact.

Jesus modeled this principle in His own life. He had "nowhere to lay his head" (Luke 9:58) and taught His disciples not to worry about material needs but to "seek first the Kingdom of God and His righteousness" (Matthew 6:33). His life was free from material entanglements, allowing Him to live with undivided devotion to the Father's will. This model challenges modern Christians to consider how excess may cloud their ability to hear from God and serve others wholeheartedly.

The early church also embraced a minimalist ethos. In Acts 2:44–45, believers "had everything in common," selling their possessions and distributing the proceeds to anyone in need. This radical simplicity was not legislated but flowed from love and a shared vision of God's Kingdom. Their lack of attachment to material goods fostered a vibrant, generous, and Spirit-filled community.

Simplicity also reflects spiritual freedom. When believers are not tethered to possessions, they become more responsive to God's leading. The more we accumulate, the more we must maintain, insure, store, and worry about. The minimalist life removes these burdens and creates space for peace, rest, and a focused pursuit of God's purposes.

Living calls for practical changes: decluttering homes, evaluating purchases, setting limits on digital and media consumption, and simplifying schedules. These deeply spiritual decisions reflect a desire to be fully available to God. Richard Foster notes in *Celebration of Discipline* that simplicity is "an inward reality that results in an outward lifestyle." When our hearts are centered on Christ, our external lives reflect that focus.

Moreover, simplicity fosters gratitude and contentment. It invites us to appreciate our blessings, rather than chasing the illusion of fulfillment through more. In doing so, we resist the cultural lie that our value is tied to our possessions and instead affirm that our identity is secure in Christ alone.

Ultimately, minimalism and simplicity are not about rules, but about alignment—with God's heart, our purpose, and the rhythms of grace. It is a life of open hands and hearts marked by freedom, generosity, and profound joy. By stewarding our lives with simplicity, we create space for more profound connection with God and greater effectiveness in our calling.

Purposeful Living: Aligning Daily Life with Kingdom Vision

Living with purpose is not merely about achieving goals or personal fulfillment; it is about orienting every area of life around the eternal purposes of God. The call to live purposefully emerges from the understanding that each day, each opportunity, and each resource is a sacred trust from the Lord. Ephesians 5:15–16 exhorts, "Be very careful, then, how you live—not as unwise but as wise, making the most of every opportunity, because the days are evil." This call challenges believers to approach life with intentionality and spiritual discernment, ensuring that our actions reflect divine priorities rather than fleeting worldly ambitions.

Purposeful living begins with clarity about our identity and calling. When believers understand who they are in Christ— redeemed, beloved, and commissioned—they can resist the pull of aimless busyness and instead live with focused intention. This means viewing daily routines, career choices, family responsibilities, and leisure through a Kingdom lens. Purpose does not reside only in extraordinary acts or public platforms; it is just as powerfully demonstrated in faithful, unseen obedience—raising children, serving in the local church, showing kindness to a neighbor, or working with integrity.

To live purposefully is also to embrace discipline. This is not a burdensome rigidity but a joyful structure that enables freedom. Spiritual disciplines such as prayer, Scripture reading, Sabbath observance, and silence help to create space for reflection, realignment, and renewal. These rhythms ground us in God's presence and keep our lives from being swept away by distraction or superficial pursuits. When our inner world is rooted in God, our outer world begins to reflect intentional purpose.

Furthermore, living purposefully involves aligning our talents, passions, and influence with God's mission in the world. Every believer has been uniquely gifted and strategically placed to make a Kingdom impact. Whether through entrepreneurship, education, creative arts, caregiving, or leadership, believers are called to steward their lives in ways that reflect the character of Christ and advance the gospel. As Paul writes in 1 Corinthians 10:31, "Whatever you do, do it all for the glory of God." This holistic view of purpose unifies all areas of life under a singular aim—to know Christ and make Him known.

Importantly, purposeful living is not about perfection but progression. It is a journey of daily surrender, listening for God's guidance, and taking faithful steps forward. Some days may feel mundane or uncertain, but the consistent choice to seek God's will and honor Him in the ordinary builds a life of extraordinary significance. This kind of living becomes a testimony to others, pointing them not to our accomplishments but to the Source of our purpose and peace.

In a world that often prizes productivity over presence and ambition over authenticity, the believer is invited into a better way—an intentional, Christ-centered, and eternally impactful life. Purposeful living is a form of stewardship, saying to God, "All that I am and all that I have is Yours. Use me as you will." When we embrace this posture, we find fulfillment and become vessels through which God's purposes flow freely into the world.

Conclusion: A Life Well Stewarded

Ultimately, stewardship is not a compartment of the Christian life—it is the Christian life. Every breath we take, every dollar we spend, every moment we invest is an opportunity to honor God and advance His Kingdom. When believers live with a deep sense of purpose and embrace simplicity, they begin to reflect the heart of the Gospel—one that is generous, selfless, and profoundly impactful.

Purposeful and simple living does not mean living small; it means living focused. It allows us to shed the burdens of consumerism, distraction, and self-centered ambition to favor a life aligned with God's mission. This is the life Jesus modeled and the life He invites us into—a life where we are faithful stewards, not frantic owners; we live open-handedly, not with clenched fists.

As we seek to steward what matters, may we remember that we are called to live not for our own name, but for the name above every name. May our lives, marked by faithfulness and simplicity, point others to the beauty of a surrendered life. Moreover, may we hear, at the end of our journey, the words of our Master: "Well done, good and faithful servant."

The Dwelling Place

Chapter 12

Grow in Influence God's Way — Leading with Humility and Spiritual Power

In the world's eyes, influence is often measured by platform, prestige, and personal advancement. However, the Kingdom of God turns such assumptions upside down. Actual influence in the eyes of God is not rooted in self-promotion or dominance, but in humble service, spiritual authority, and Christlike character. Jesus modeled an entirely different paradigm of leadership—one in which influence flows from obedience, integrity, and dependence on the Holy Spirit.

The believer is not called to reject influence but to steward it God's way. Every follower of Christ has a sphere of influence—whether in family, ministry, community, or the marketplace. The question is not whether we will lead, but how we will lead. This chapter explores what it means to grow in godly influence, examining the character, posture, and practices distinguishing Kingdom leaders from worldly ones.

Influence Begins with Integrity: The Foundation of Godly Leadership

At the core of Kingdom influence lies integrity, which is the alignment of character and conduct with the truth of God's Word. Scripture reminds us that "A good name is more desirable

175

than great riches" (Prov. 22:1). In an age of image management and superficial charisma, integrity sustains lasting influence.

Integrity is not developed in public but cultivated in private. It is formed in the hidden places, through decisions made when no one is watching, in the quiet surrender to God when compromise tempts, and in the steadfast commitment to truth when lies seem convenient. Daniel in Babylon demonstrated such integrity. Faced with the temptation to conform, he "resolved not to defile himself" (Dan. 1:8). His private convictions laid the groundwork for his public influence.

Jesus' own leadership was marked by flawless integrity. He never compromised truth for popularity. His words and actions were perfectly aligned with the Father's will (John 8:29). His followers, therefore, are called to the same unwavering commitment to righteousness. As Proverbs 11:3 declares, "The integrity of the upright guides them, but their duplicity destroys the unfaithful."

Influence that lacks integrity is fragile and fleeting. The world is filled with gifted leaders whose platforms collapsed under the weight of moral failure. In contrast, godly influence grows from a life hidden in Christ, where private devotion produces public credibility. As the psalmist prayed, "May integrity and uprightness protect me, because my hope, LORD, is in you" (Ps. 25:21).

John Maxwell affirms this truth when he notes, "Leadership is influence, nothing more, nothing less"—but that influence rests on the foundation of character and consistency.[98]

---

[98] John C. Maxwell, *The 21 Irrefutable Laws of Leadership* (Nashville: Thomas Nelson, 2007), 56

Maxwell explains that influence built without integrity is like a house without a foundation—it may look impressive for a season, but inevitably, cracks will appear, and collapse will follow.

Moreover, integrity builds trust—and trust is the currency of influence. People may follow talent temporarily, but they follow character for a lifetime. Integrity allows leaders to weather criticism, overcome opposition, and maintain credibility in the face of failure or misunderstanding.

Kingdom leaders do not pursue perfection, but authenticity. They acknowledge weaknesses, repent of failures, and pursue accountability. In doing so, they model integrity not as flawless performance but as consistent alignment with truth and humility before God.

Servanthood Over Self-Promotion: The Posture of Kingdom Leaders

Jesus shattered conventional notions of leadership when He declared, "Whoever wants to become great among you must be your servant" (Matt. 20:26). In the Kingdom, greatness is not reserved for the ambitious but for the humble. True influence flows not from self-promotion but from sacrificial service.

This servant-hearted posture was exemplified when Jesus washed His disciples' feet—an act unthinkable for someone recognized as "Lord and Teacher" (John 13:14). Yet in this simple, humbling gesture, He demonstrated that leadership is not about status, but about stooping low to lift others.

Henry and Richard Blackaby describe this as "moving people onto God's agenda," not our own.[99] Godly leaders embrace servanthood, not as a temporary strategy, but as a lifestyle. Whether in ministry, business, or the home, they use their influence to empower, equip, and encourage those under their care. They are not driven by ego but by compassion and a desire to reflect Christ.

Servant leadership, however, is not weakness—it requires courage, humility, and resilience. It calls leaders to lay down their rights for the sake of others and to seek the flourishing of those they lead, even at personal cost.

The life of the Apostle Paul models this Kingdom posture. Though entrusted with authority, Paul consistently referred to himself as a servant of Christ (Rom. 1:1) and laid down his own rights to serve others (1 Cor. 9:19). His leadership was not self-serving but sacrificial, aimed at building up the church.

Furthermore, servant leadership elevates others rather than oneself. It rejoices in the success, growth, and promotion of those being led. It creates space for new leaders to emerge, recognizing that the goal of influence is not control but multiplication. Jesus spent three years pouring into His disciples so they would surpass His earthly ministry, declaring, "Very truly I tell you, whoever believes in me will do the works I have been doing, and they will do even greater things" (John 14:12).

In practical terms, servant leadership looks like listening more than speaking, encouraging more than criticizing, and giving more than receiving. It requires leaders to be present,

---

[99] Henry and Richard Blackaby, *Spiritual Leadership: Moving People to God's Agenda* (Nashville: B&H Publishing, 2011), 73

approachable, and willing to do the unnoticed tasks. It means valuing people over projects and relationships over results.

In a culture obsessed with self-promotion, the servant-hearted leader stands in stark contrast. Their influence is not fueled by flashy platforms but by quiet, consistent service that earns trust and fosters transformation. Theirs is the influence that endures, for it mirrors the very heart of the Servant King.

The Spirit's Empowerment: Source of Lasting Influence

Kingdom influence is never self-generated. It is the fruit of a life surrendered to and empowered by the Holy Spirit. Jesus commanded His disciples to wait for the Spirit before embarking on their mission, declaring, "You will receive power when the Holy Spirit comes on you; and you will be my witnesses" (Acts 1:8).

Influence apart from the Spirit produces temporary results, but influence rooted in the Spirit transforms lives and advances the Kingdom. Paul affirmed this when he wrote, "Our gospel came to you not simply with words but also with power, with the Holy Spirit and deep conviction" (1 Thess. 1:5).

The Spirit empowers leaders with wisdom, courage, discernment, and spiritual authority. They are equipped to speak truth, demonstrate love, confront injustice, and model Christlike character through Him. The Spirit also produces fruit in their lives—qualities like love, patience, and self-control—that enhance their credibility and effectiveness.

Dallas Willard reminds us that "the fruit of the Kingdom is never produced by mere human effort, but by abiding in the reality of God's reign."[100] This abiding relationship with the Spirit is not a mystical experience reserved for a few, but the daily posture of every believer surrendered to Christ.

Throughout Scripture, we see how Spirit-empowered leaders changed the course of history. In Acts 4:31, after praying, the early church was filled with the Holy Spirit and boldly spoke the word of God. Their influence was not a product of eloquence but of divine empowerment. The Apostle Paul, though physically unimpressive by worldly standards (2 Cor. 10:10), shook cities and nations through Spirit-led ministry. His courage, endurance, and spiritual authority were rooted not in personality but in the Holy Spirit.

Moreover, the Spirit's empowerment protects leaders from burnout and striving. Human effort alone cannot sustain lasting influence. Even Jesus ministered "in the power of the Spirit" (Luke 4:14), demonstrating the necessity of divine enablement. Leaders dependent on the Spirit find renewed strength, divine wisdom, and supernatural grace for every assignment.

Spirit-empowered leaders also carry spiritual discernment. They perceive beyond surface issues, recognizing spiritual strongholds and opportunities for Kingdom advancement. Both boldness and humility, truth and grace, courage and compassion mark their influence.

Cultivating a Spirit-empowered life requires intentionality. It begins with daily surrender, inviting the Spirit to lead, correct, and empower. It is nurtured through prayer,

---

[100] Dallas Willard, *The Divine Conspiracy: Rediscovering Our Hidden Life in God* (San Francisco: HarperOne, 2009), 258.

fasting, worship, and obedience. The more leaders depend on the Spirit, the greater their influence—not in worldly fame, but in eternal, transformational impact.

Building Influence Through Relationships, Not Control

Influence in the Kingdom is relational, not positional. Jesus modeled this by investing deeply in twelve disciples, teaching, correcting, and loving them into maturity. His influence was not based on coercion but on connection.

Godly leaders understand that authority is most effective when rooted in relationship. They build trust through consistency, care, and authentic communication. Paul exemplified this with the Thessalonian church, writing, "We were gentle among you, like a nursing mother caring for her children...because you had become so dear to us" (1 Thess. 2:7–8).

In contrast to worldly leadership that relies on fear or manipulation, Kingdom influence flows from love, service, and genuine concern for others' growth. Healthy relationships become the soil in which influence takes root and multiplies.

Jesus' entire leadership model revolved around relationships. He chose to walk closely with His disciples, sharing meals, hardships, and even moments of weakness, such as His agony in Gethsemane. His authority was not built on hierarchy, but on proximity, compassion, and consistent investment.

Building relational influence requires intentionality. It demands that leaders slow down, listen well, and prioritize connection over control. Rather than issuing commands from a distance, godly leaders walk alongside those they lead, offering encouragement, correction, and support.

Relational leadership fosters an atmosphere of safety where vulnerability is welcomed, and trust can flourish. In such environments, people are empowered to grow, take risks, and reach their potential. Leaders who value relationships over control do not fear others' success; they celebrate and cultivate it.

Moreover, relational influence is sustainable. Positional authority may compel obedience temporarily, but love and trust inspire long-term loyalty and transformation. As J. Oswald Sanders emphasizes, "Spiritual leadership is not won by promotion but by many prayers and tears."[101] True influence is forged in the context of authentic relationships, not hierarchical structures.

Practically, this means leaders prioritize mentorship, discipleship, and collaboration. They seek to know the hopes, struggles, and gifts of those they lead. They offer correction with grace, celebrate progress, and remain approachable even in positions of authority.

Ultimately, Kingdom influence grows not through control but through Christlike love expressed in relationship. As leaders model the relational heart of Jesus, they cultivate environments where influence is multiplied and lives are transformed for God's glory.

---

[101] J. Oswald Sanders, *Spiritual Leadership: Principles of Excellence for Every Believer* (Chicago: Moody Publishers, 2007), 112.

Influence Tested Through Trials: How God Refines Leaders

Every leader's influence will be tested. Trials, opposition, and seasons of obscurity reveal the depth of one's character and the source of one's influence. Scripture consistently shows that God refines leaders through difficulty before entrusting them with greater responsibility.

Joseph endured betrayal, false accusation, and imprisonment before ascending to leadership in Egypt (Gen. 37–41). David faced rejection, hiding, and warfare before being crowned king (1 Sam. 16–2 Sam. 5). Even Jesus was "made perfect through suffering" (Heb. 2:10).

Throughout church history, some of the most influential leaders have emerged from seasons of intense testing. The Apostle Paul, for example, suffered beatings, shipwreck, imprisonment, and persecution, yet these trials refined his faith and expanded his spiritual authority (2 Cor. 11:23–28). His hardships produced a depth of character and a credibility that words alone could never convey.

Trials test motives, reveal hidden weaknesses, and cultivate humility. They expose whether a leader's influence is rooted in ambition or surrendered to God's purposes. Leaders who emerge from adversity with greater dependency on God and refined character become more effective and trustworthy influencers.

Furthermore, trials develop resilience and perseverance. James exhorts, "Let perseverance finish its work so that you may be mature and complete, not lacking anything" (James 1:4). Trials strip away self-sufficiency and invite leaders into deeper intimacy with God, where strength is renewed, and wisdom is gained.

Seasons of obscurity—where one's gifts go unnoticed and influence feels limited—are equally formative. Moses spent forty years in the wilderness before stepping into his calling. Jesus lived thirty years in quiet obedience before beginning His public ministry. These hidden seasons cultivate patience, character, and unwavering trust in God's timing.

Leaders refined through trials do not resent adversity; they embrace it as God's refining fire. They understand that true influence is not a result of platform but of perseverance, not of charisma but of character.

In the Kingdom, influence is not microwaved but slow-cooked in the furnace of testing. Those willing to endure God's refining process emerge as trustworthy vessels of His power, equipped to lead with humility, wisdom, and spiritual authority.

Stewarding Influence for God's Glory, Not Personal Gain

Influence is a stewardship, not a trophy. Kingdom leaders understand that all influence ultimately belongs to God and exists for His purposes. As Paul declared, "What do you have that you did not receive?" (1 Cor. 4:7).

This perspective guards against pride, entitlement, and exploitation. Leaders with a Kingdom mindset steward their influence to advance the gospel, promote justice, and equip others—not to build personal empires.

Stewarding influence well involves humility, accountability, and a constant check of motives. Leaders submit to spiritual oversight, welcome correction, and continually surrender their ambitions to Christ. They recognize that influence is not for personal gain but for God's mission. As Jesus warned, "From everyone who has been given much, much will be demanded" (Luke 12:48).

A.W. Tozer writes, "The man who has God for his treasure has all things."[102] True Kingdom influence is sustained only when leaders keep their hearts fixed on God, not personal recognition. The moment influence becomes an idol rather than an instrument, it corrupts both the leader and those they lead.

In practical terms, stewarding influence means evaluating how authority, platforms, and opportunities are being used. Are they promoting self or pointing to Christ? Are they advancing God's Kingdom or building personal kingdoms? Wise leaders surround themselves with mentors and accountability structures to safeguard their hearts and ensure that their influence serves the greater good.

Additionally, stewarding influence involves a willingness to give it away. True leaders are not possessive but generative. They raise up others, empower emerging leaders, and rejoice when influence multiplies beyond themselves. Like John the Baptist, they humbly declare, "He must become greater; I must become less" (John 3:30).

Stewardship also requires recognizing seasons. Influence may ebb and flow according to God's timing. Wise leaders are not obsessed with maintaining status but are content to lead,

---

[102] A.W. Tozer, *The Pursuit of God* (Harrisburg: Christian Publications, 1982), 84

serve, or step aside as the Spirit directs. Their identity is rooted not in influence but in their relationship with Christ.

When influence is stewarded for God's glory, it becomes a powerful tool for Kingdom impact—bringing hope to the broken, mobilizing the church, and pointing others to Jesus. Such influence outlasts platforms, positions, and applause, echoing into eternity for the glory of God.

Conclusion: Becoming a Leader Who Reflects Christ

The ultimate model for influence is not a celebrity, CEO, or political figure—but Jesus Christ, the Servant-King. His life, death, and resurrection redefined greatness, power, and leadership. Believers are called to grow in influence, not for self-glorification but to reflect Christ and expand His Kingdom. Whether leading a church, a business, a family, or simply living faithfully daily, every follower of Jesus can lead with humility, serve with love, and influence others for God's glory.

Kingdom influence begins with integrity, grows through servanthood, is empowered by the Spirit, is rooted in relationships, refined by trials, and stewarded for God's purposes. As believers embrace this calling, they become leaders who make a difference and reflect Christ's heart in every sphere of influence.

Chapter 13

Step Forward in Bold Faith: Living with Courage and Kingdom Confidence

From the beginning of biblical history, God's work on earth has been accomplished not through the most powerful, wealthy, or influential by worldly standards, but through ordinary men and women willing to embrace extraordinary courage. Bold faith has always been the distinguishing mark of those used mightily by God. It is the catalyst that propels believers beyond the confines of fear, comfort, and self-preservation into the vast possibilities of Kingdom living.

Throughout the Old and New Testaments, we find that God's Kingdom advances through individuals who respond to His call with audacious faith. Noah, Abraham, Moses, Ruth, David, Mary, and the Apostles all faced moments where fear could have kept them stagnant, yet they pressed forward with confidence rooted in the character of God. Bold faith is not reckless enthusiasm; it is grounded in a settled conviction that God's promises are sure, His presence is constant, and His power is sufficient.

In the twenty-first century, the need for bold faith is more pressing than ever. The cultural currents of compromise, fear, and passivity threaten to neutralize believers' effectiveness. Moral relativism, social pressures, and increasing hostility toward biblical truth create an environment where many are tempted to remain silent or passive. However, Scripture calls the Church not to shrink back in timidity but to rise in unwavering confidence, empowered by the Spirit and anchored in God's promises. The advancement of God's purposes requires believers willing to step forward in bold, unwavering faith.

Hebrews 11, often called the "Hall of Faith," provides a sweeping account of men and women whose audacious trust in God altered the course of history. From Abraham's journey into the unknown to Esther's courageous stand before a king, Scripture reveals that bold faith is not an optional characteristic for select spiritual elites—it is the expected posture of every follower of Christ. Their stories remind us that bold faith is rarely comfortable but always transformational.

This chapter explores the theological foundations, biblical models, obstacles, and practical pathways for cultivating bold faith. Through sound doctrine, scriptural insight, and spiritual disciplines, believers can develop the courage necessary to live as confident ambassadors of Christ in a world desperate for the light of the Gospel. In doing so, they fulfill their Kingdom purpose and reflect the boldness of Christ Himself.

The Nature of Bold, Biblical Faith

At its core, bold faith is not a personality trait or a product of human willpower; it is rooted in a proper understanding of God. Biblical faith is the settled confidence that God is who He says He is and will do what He has promised. It flows from knowledge of God's character—His sovereignty, faithfulness, goodness, and power. True courage arises not from self-assurance but from God-assurance.

The Apostle Paul reminds believers that "faith comes from hearing, and hearing through the word of Christ" (Rom. 10:17). A robust faith develops as one's understanding of God deepens through engagement with Scripture. As theologian J.I. Packer asserts, "The root of Christian faith is revelation—God making Himself known."[103] The more believers grasp God's self-revelation, the more their faith is fortified.

Moreover, bold faith is intrinsically connected to the believer's identity in Christ. The New Testament declares that those in Christ are "more than conquerors" (Rom. 8:37), "a royal priesthood" (1 Pet. 2:9), and "ambassadors for Christ" (2 Cor. 5:20). This identity provides the foundation for courage, assuring believers that their position in the Kingdom is secure, their authority is derived from Christ, and their ultimate victory is guaranteed.

Understanding the believer's identity in Christ reshapes how we view opposition and difficulty. Bold faith acknowledges that suffering and resistance are inevitable for those who follow Jesus, but it affirms that no trial can thwart God's purposes. The Apostle Peter declared, "But even if you should suffer for righteousness' sake, you will be blessed. Have no fear of them, nor be troubled" (1 Pet. 3:14). This perspective fuels unwavering boldness even in the face of uncertainty.

The doctrine of the Holy Spirit's indwelling presence also undergirds bold faith. Jesus promised His followers that the Spirit would empower them to be His witnesses (Acts 1:8). The book of Acts records the fulfillment of this promise as ordinary

---

[103] Joseph Pieper, *The Four Cardinal Virtues* (Notre Dame, IN: University of Notre Dame Press, 1966), 128.

believers, filled with the Spirit, proclaimed the Gospel with courage, performed miracles, and endured persecution with unwavering resolve. The same Spirit who emboldened the early Church resides within every believer today, providing supernatural power to live courageously.

Additionally, the promises of God form a stabilizing anchor for bold faith. Throughout Scripture, God's faithfulness is consistently displayed, reminding His people that He is trustworthy. Joshua declared to Israel, "Not one word has failed of all the good things that the Lord your God promised concerning you" (Josh. 23:14). When believers fix their gaze on the unchanging promises of God, bold faith becomes the logical response.

Thus, bold faith is not the product of natural confidence or spiritual arrogance. It is a Spirit-enabled, Scripture-grounded, Christ-centered trust that propels believers into courageous obedience, regardless of circumstances. It is sustained not by emotional fervor but by deep theological conviction. As believers anchor their lives in God's truth, they are equipped to step forward in bold faith, becoming instruments of Kingdom impact in a hesitant world.

Biblical Portraits of Courageous Faith

Scripture provides many examples of men and women who exhibited remarkable bold faith in the face of uncertainty, opposition, and impossible odds. Their stories inspire and provide timeless blueprints for believers today seeking to cultivate unwavering confidence in God.

Abraham, revered as the "father of faith," epitomizes courageous obedience. Called by God to leave his homeland and journey to an unknown destination, Abraham departed "not knowing where he was going" (Heb. 11:8). His willingness to step into uncertainty, trusting solely in God's promises, established a model of bold faith that echoes throughout redemptive history.

Esther, a young Jewish woman elevated to the position of queen in Persia, faced a defining moment when her people were threatened with annihilation. Risking her life by approaching the king uninvited, Esther declared, "If I perish, I perish" (Est. 4:16). Her boldness was not born of self-preservation but of unwavering trust in God's providence.

David's confrontation with Goliath is perhaps one of the most iconic demonstrations of bold faith. While the armies of Israel cowered in fear, David stepped onto the battlefield armed not with military prowess but with confidence in "the name of the Lord Almighty" (1 Sam. 17:45). His declaration, "The battle is the Lord's," reflects the essence of bold faith—reliance not on human strength, but on divine power.

In the New Testament, the Apostles exemplified Spirit-empowered boldness. Despite threats, imprisonment, and persecution, they proclaimed the Gospel with courage and conviction. Acts records that "when they saw the boldness of Peter and John," the religious leaders "recognized that they had been with Jesus" (Acts 4:13). Their courage flowed from intimacy with Christ and empowerment by the Holy Spirit.

These biblical examples reveal that bold faith is not reserved for the fearless or naturally assertive. It is cultivated in ordinary people who choose to trust an extraordinary God. Their stories remind believers that boldness is not the absence of fear but the triumph of faith over fear—a willingness to act despite uncertainty, confident in God's character and promises.

Common Obstacles to Bold Faith

Despite the clear biblical mandate and inspiring examples, cultivating bold faith is not without challenges. Every believer faces internal and external obstacles that can hinder the development of courageous trust in God. Recognizing these barriers is essential to overcoming them and stepping forward in obedience.

One of the most common obstacles to bold faith is fear—fear of failure, rejection, inadequacy, or loss. Fear is a powerful emotion that, when left unchecked, paralyzes believers and prevents them from pursuing God's calling. Scripture repeatedly addresses this reality, offering reassurance and exhortation. God declared to Joshua, "Have I not commanded you? Be strong and courageous. Do not be afraid; do not be discouraged, for the Lord your God will be with you wherever you go" (Josh. 1:9). The presence of fear is not sinful in itself; rather, it is the response to fear that determines the outcome.

Doubt is another significant obstacle. Even the most devoted followers of Christ can wrestle with moments of uncertainty, questioning God's promises or their own abilities. Peter's experience walking on water illustrates this tension. As long as Peter fixed his gaze on Jesus, he walked above the waves. However, when doubt crept in, he began to sink (Matt. 14:28-31). Jesus' response, "You of little faith, why did you doubt?" highlights how doubt undermines boldness and reinforces the importance of steadfast focus on Christ.

Past wounds and failures can also erode confidence. Believers who have experienced disappointment, betrayal, or perceived spiritual shortcomings may hesitate to step out in faith again. The enemy exploits these experiences, sowing lies of inadequacy and unworthiness. However, God's grace is sufficient to heal and restore. The Apostle Paul, despite his past as a persecutor of the Church, became one of the boldest proclaimers of the Gospel. His life testifies that God's power is made perfect in human weakness (2 Cor. 12:9).

Cultural pressures and societal opposition often discourage believers from living boldly for Christ. In an increasingly secular world, standing for biblical truth can invite ridicule, marginalization, or even persecution. The fear of losing reputation, relationships, or opportunities tempts many to compromise or remain silent. However, Jesus warned that following Him would come with a cost (Matt. 10:22). Bold faith requires a resolve to honor God above public approval.

Comfort and complacency also undermine boldness. The desire for safety, ease, and predictability can dull spiritual fervor and limit risk-taking for the Kingdom. The parable of the talents illustrates this principle. The servant who buried his talent out of fear and complacency was rebuked, while those who invested and multiplied their resources were commended (Matt. 25:14-30). Stepping forward in bold faith necessitates leaving comfort zones and embracing Kingdom adventure.

Finally, spiritual apathy and neglect of spiritual disciplines weaken the foundation of bold faith. Prayerlessness, disengagement from Scripture, and isolation from Christian community erode the inner strength required for courageous living. The early Church's boldness flowed from persistent prayer, devotion to the Word, and mutual encouragement (Acts 2:42-47; 4:31).

Overcoming these obstacles requires intentionality, dependence on the Holy Spirit, and continual renewal of the mind through God's Word. By identifying and addressing these barriers, believers position themselves to cultivate the kind of bold, unwavering faith that honors God and advances His Kingdom.

Cultivating Boldness Through Spiritual Disciplines

Bold faith is not merely the byproduct of personality or natural courage—it is cultivated through intentional spiritual formation. The disciplines of the Christian life are God's gracious tools for shaping the heart, renewing the mind, and strengthening the believer's confidence in Him.

Prayer is the first and most essential discipline for developing bold faith. Time spent in the presence of God fuels spiritual courage. In the book of Acts, the early believers, facing threats and opposition, "raised their voices together in prayer to God" (Acts 4:24). Their petition was not for safety or comfort, but for boldness: "Enable your servants to speak your word with great boldness" (Acts 4:29). God's response was immediate: "They were all filled with the Holy Spirit and spoke the word of God boldly" (Acts 4:31). Consistent prayer realigns the believer's heart with God's purposes and imparts supernatural courage.

Meditation on Scripture is another indispensable discipline for cultivating boldness. The Word of God reveals His character, promises, and faithfulness throughout history. Joshua was commanded to "meditate on it day and night" (Josh. 1:8) so that he would have the courage to lead Israel into the Promised

Land. The psalms, the prophets, the Gospels, and the epistles all testify to God's unfailing power and provision for those who trust Him.

Worship also strengthens bold faith. Declaring the greatness of God lifts the believer's perspective beyond present fears and reminds them of the Almighty One who reigns above all. Worship reinforces the truth that "if God is for us, who can be against us?" (Rom. 8:31).

Fasting fosters humility and dependence on God, clarifying spiritual vision and exposing areas of fear or complacency that hinder boldness. Community and fellowship provide accountability, encouragement, and the shared strength of other believers who are also pursuing courageous obedience.

Serving others stretches faith by requiring believers to step beyond self-interest and comfort zones. Acts of generosity, hospitality, evangelism, and compassion create opportunities to rely on God's strength rather than human ability.

These spiritual disciplines are not legalistic obligations but life-giving practices that cultivate the conditions for bold faith to flourish. They root the believer in God's truth, align the heart with His purposes, and provide the supernatural resources necessary to step forward in obedience with unwavering confidence.

The Holy Spirit: Source of Lasting Boldness

The ultimate source of bold faith is not found in human strength, personality, or willpower, but in the indwelling presence and power of the Holy Spirit. Jesus, recognizing the fear and uncertainty His disciples would face, promised them the Holy Spirit as their Helper, Comforter, and Empowerer (John 14:16-17).

At Pentecost, this promise was fulfilled as the Holy Spirit descended upon the believers, transforming a once fearful, hesitant group into bold, courageous witnesses (Acts 2). Peter, who had previously denied Jesus out of fear, stood and proclaimed the Gospel with unwavering authority, resulting in thousands coming to faith (Acts 2:14-41).

The book of Acts continually testifies to the Spirit's role in producing boldness. When faced with threats and persecution, the early believers did not shrink back but prayed for greater boldness, and "they were all filled with the Holy Spirit and spoke the word of God boldly" (Acts 4:31).

The same Holy Spirit who empowered the early Church resides within every believer today. He equips, guides, convicts, and emboldens followers of Christ to stand firm in truth, resist fear, and advance the Kingdom with confidence.

The Spirit's empowerment is not reserved for moments of crisis or public ministry; it is available for daily life. Whether sharing one's faith with a friend, standing for righteousness in the workplace, confronting injustice, or persevering through trials, the Holy Spirit infuses the believer with supernatural courage.

Cultivating an ongoing relationship with the Holy Spirit through prayer, surrender, and obedience is essential for living a bold, Kingdom-centered life. As believers yield to His leading, they discover a boldness that transcends human limitations and reflects the unstoppable power of God.

The Kingdom Impact of Bold Faith

The fruit of bold faith is not merely personal spiritual growth but measurable advancement of God's Kingdom purposes on earth. Throughout Scripture and Church history, courageous obedience has been the catalyst for evangelism, revival, societal transformation, and generational legacy.

Bold faith fuels evangelistic witness. The early Church in Acts multiplied rapidly, not because of slick marketing or cultural compromise, but through Spirit-empowered believers proclaiming the Gospel boldly in the face of opposition. Even when commanded to remain silent, the apostles replied, "We cannot help speaking about what we have seen and heard" (Acts 4:20).

Throughout history, men and women who stepped forward in bold faith have sparked missionary movements that carried the Gospel to unreached peoples. William Carey, known as the "father of modern missions," defied cultural skepticism and launched a global missions movement, declaring, "Expect great things from God; attempt great things for God." His bold faith changed the spiritual trajectory of nations.

Bold faith also brings healing and restoration to brokenness in the world. Jesus commissioned His followers to "preach the Kingdom of God and heal the sick" (Luke 9:2). Today, bold prayers of faith release God's power to bring physical healing, emotional restoration, and deliverance from spiritual bondage.

Courageous faith confronts injustice and champions righteousness. Biblical heroes like Moses, Esther, and Daniel stood boldly against corrupt systems, risking comfort and safety to advance God's justice. Modern examples include the abolitionist efforts of William Wilberforce and the civil rights leadership of Dr. Martin Luther King Jr.—both driven by bold, Kingdom-rooted faith.

Within the Church, bold faith cultivates unity, generosity, and supernatural community. Fear breeds division and self-preservation, but boldness rooted in Christ produces sacrificial love, radical hospitality, and contagious hope that draws others to Jesus.

Bold faith also strengthens future generations. When parents, mentors, and spiritual leaders model courageous obedience, they inspire those they influence to do likewise. Timothy's boldness was shaped by the faith of his grandmother Lois and mother Eunice (2 Tim. 1:5).

Ultimately, bold faith glorifies God by making His power and goodness visible in the world. As Jesus declared, "Let your light shine before others, that they may see your good deeds and glorify your Father in heaven" (Matt. 5:16).

The Kingdom impact of bold faith ripples far beyond individual lives. It transforms families, churches, communities, and nations, advancing God's purposes and establishing a legacy that endures for eternity.

Conclusion: Living as Courageous Kingdom Ambassadors

The call to step forward in bold faith is not reserved for spiritual heroes or historical figures—it is the daily invitation extended to every follower of Christ. Regardless of background, personality, or past failures, every believer is equipped and empowered to walk in courageous obedience through the indwelling presence of the Holy Spirit.

Bold faith does not require the absence of fear but the willingness to act despite it. It begins with a settled trust in the character and promises of God and is sustained through the daily disciplines of prayer, Scripture engagement, worship, and Spirit-filled community.

The examples of Abraham, Esther, David, the apostles, and countless others remind us that bold faith changes history. It opens doors for evangelism, confronts injustice, fosters unity within the Church, and leaves a lasting legacy for generations to come. However, bold faith is ultimately not about personal accomplishment or recognition but glorifying God and advancing His Kingdom. As we confidently step forward, we participate in His unfolding redemptive plan for the world.

In these challenging and uncertain times, the Church does not need more passive observers or timid bystanders. The world is desperate for courageous men and women who will rise in faith, proclaim the Gospel with boldness, serve with sacrificial love, and stand firm for righteousness. May we be those people. May we cultivate bold faith not for our own comfort or success, but for the glory of God and the advancement of His Kingdom. Moreover, when we falter, may we return to His presence, be filled afresh with His Spirit, and step forward once more in unwavering, bold faith.

As the writer of Hebrews exhorts: "But we do not belong to those who shrink back and are destroyed, but to those who have faith and are saved" (Heb. 10:39).

Let us live as courageous Kingdom ambassadors, fully persuaded that the God who calls us is faithful to accomplish His purposes through us.

Chapter 14

Shine and Share the Gospel: Living as a Kingdom Witness

The call to share the gospel is central to the mission of every believer. It is not merely a recommendation nor an optional aspect of Christian discipleship; it is an essential part of our identity in Christ. Jesus clearly instructed His followers, "Go into all the world and proclaim the gospel to the whole creation" (Mark 16:15). This command encompasses more than simply speaking words—it involves a lifestyle that vividly demonstrates the gospel's transformative power.

The biblical vision of evangelism is firmly rooted in God's redemptive nature. As Christopher J. H. Wright notes, "It is not so much the case that God has a mission for His church in the world as that God has a church for His mission in the world."[104] The very essence of God's character as a sending God compels believers to participate in His ongoing mission of reconciliation (2 Cor. 5:18-20).

---

[104] Christopher J. H. Wright, *The Mission of God: Unlocking the Bible's Grand Narrative* (Downers Grove, IL: IVP Academic, 2006), 62

To shine as Kingdom witnesses means embodying the truth, love, and power of Jesus Christ in every area of life. Just as Jesus described His followers as "the light of the world" (Matt. 5:14), our lives are intended to illuminate the darkness around us, pointing others toward the hope found in Christ alone. This shining is not passive or subtle—it is intentional, courageous, and unmistakably marked by love, grace, and humility.

Lesslie Newbigin emphasizes the importance of embodied witness, arguing that "the only hermeneutic of the gospel is a congregation that believes it and lives by it."[105] In an increasingly pluralistic and skeptical world, the credibility of our message hinges not only on the clarity of our words but on the consistency and authenticity of our lives.

Moreover, gospel witnessing does not come from human effort alone but from the empowerment of the Holy Spirit. As John Stott observes, "The Spirit of God leads the people of God to engage in the mission of God."[106] By God's enabling, believers can boldly proclaim and demonstrate the hope of salvation.

This chapter explores how believers can practically and powerfully shine as Kingdom ambassadors, effectively sharing the gospel through word and deed. We will examine the theological foundations of gospel witness, compelling biblical examples, common challenges, and practical strategies for cultivating a vibrant, influential testimony in today's world.

Theological Foundations of Gospel Witness

---

[105] Lesslie Newbigin, *The Gospel in a Pluralist Society* (Grand Rapids, MI: Eerdmans, 1989), 227

[106] John Stott, *The Radical Disciple* (Downers Grove, IL: InterVarsity Press, 2010), 88

Gospel witness is fundamentally grounded in the character and mission of God, as revealed throughout Scripture. At its core, witnessing flows not from human initiative alone but from God's redemptive purposes for all creation. The Triune God—Father, Son, and Holy Spirit—exists as a sending God, drawing humanity into relationship and commissioning His people to proclaim the message of salvation.

The theological foundation of witness begins in the Old Testament, where God's covenant with Abraham includes the promise that "all peoples on earth will be blessed through you" (Gen. 12:3). This blessing is ultimately fulfilled in Jesus Christ, whose life, death, and resurrection secure redemption for all who believe (Gal. 3:8, 13-14).

Central to gospel witness is the Incarnation—the profound truth that God became flesh in Jesus Christ (John 1:14). As theologian Michael Bird explains, "In the incarnation, God's mission is embodied, God's love is made visible, and God's saving work is inaugurated."[107] Jesus' earthly ministry models how gospel witness is proclaimed and demonstrated through acts of compassion, justice, and truth.

Christ's cross and resurrection form the gospel message's theological heart. Paul declares, "Christ died for our sins in accordance with the Scriptures... he was buried... he was raised on the third day" (1 Cor. 15:3-4). Through His atoning death and victorious resurrection, Christ reconciles humanity to God, providing the only way to salvation (John 14:6).

---

[107] Michael F. Bird, *Evangelical Theology: A Biblical and Systematic Introduction*, 2nd ed. (Grand Rapids, MI: Zondervan Academic, 2020), 509

The Holy Spirit empowers gospel witness. Jesus promised, "You will receive power when the Holy Spirit has come upon you, and you will be my witnesses" (Acts 1:8). The Spirit enables believers to proclaim the gospel with boldness, equips them with spiritual gifts, and convicts hearts, making effective witness possible.

Moreover, the Church is God's instrument for advancing His mission. The gathered community of believers is called to reflect Christ's unity, love, and holiness, serving as a "city set on a hill" (Matt. 5:14-16). As Christopher Wright affirms, "The church does not have a mission. God's mission has a church."[108]

Gospel witness is thus not optional but intrinsic to the believer's identity. It arises from experiencing God's grace and participating in His redemptive work. Rooted in God's nature, empowered by the Spirit, and expressed through the church, effective witness reflects God's love and truth to a watching world.

Biblical Models of Effective Witness

Scripture provides rich and instructive models for effective gospel witness, offering practical examples for contemporary believers seeking to share their faith with clarity and boldness. These biblical figures reveal that witnessing involves proclaiming truth and embodying compassion, cultural sensitivity, and Spirit-empowered courage.

The Apostle Paul is one of the most compelling models of effective witness. His missionary journeys and epistles

---

[108] Christopher J. H. Wright, *The Mission of God's People: A Biblical Theology of the Church's Mission* (Grand Rapids, MI: Zondervan, 2010), 25

demonstrate an unwavering commitment to proclaiming Christ while carefully contextualizing the message. In Acts 17, Paul engages with the philosophers of Athens, affirming their religious search and introducing them to "the God who made the world and everything in it" (Acts 17:24). As Eckhard Schnabel observes, "Paul's missionary strategy in Athens reflects both theological conviction and cultural intelligence."[109] His example underscores the importance of understanding one's audience while remaining faithful to the gospel.

The Samaritan woman at the well (John 4:1-42) illustrates the power of personal testimony. Her encounter with Jesus radically transformed her life, prompting her to share her story with her entire community: "Come, see a man who told me everything I ever did" (John 4:29). Her authentic witness, grounded in personal experience rather than theological expertise, led many to believe in Christ. As D. A. Carson notes, "Authentic personal encounter with Jesus naturally overflows into joyful, persuasive testimony."[110]

Peter's bold proclamation at Pentecost (Acts 2:14-41) highlights the role of Spirit-empowered witness. Filled with the Holy Spirit, Peter fearlessly declared the death, resurrection, and lordship of Christ, calling his audience to repentance and faith. The result was astonishing—about three thousand were added to their number that day. This event demonstrates that effective witness depends not on human eloquence but on the Holy Spirit's enabling power (Acts 1:8).

---

[109] Eckhard J. Schnabel, *Paul the Missionary: Realities, Strategies, and Methods* (Downers Grove, IL: IVP Academic, 2008), 306
[110] D. A. Carson, *The Gospel According to John* (Leicester, England: Inter-Varsity Press; Grand Rapids, MI: Eerdmans, 1991), 225

Stephen, the first Christian martyr, embodies courageous witness in the face of opposition (Acts 6–7). Even when confronted by hostile religious leaders, Stephen boldly proclaimed the truth of Christ, culminating in a heavenly vision and a Christ-like prayer for his persecutors. His example reminds believers that effective witness may require costly sacrifice but bears eternal fruit (Acts 7:55-60).

Finally, Philip's encounter with the Ethiopian eunuch (Acts 8:26-40) underscores the importance of Spirit-led, Scripture-centered witness. Sensitive to the Holy Spirit's prompting, Philip approached the eunuch, explained the gospel from Isaiah, and baptized him upon his confession of faith. As Craig Keener highlights, "Philip's readiness and reliance on Scripture exemplify effective evangelism in the early church."[111]

These biblical models collectively illustrate that effective witness requires courage, cultural awareness, personal authenticity, reliance on the Holy Spirit, and deep grounding in Scripture. By learning from these examples, believers today are better equipped to fulfill their calling as Kingdom witnesses in diverse and often challenging contexts.

Common Challenges in Sharing the Gospel

Despite the biblical clarity and examples that underscore the importance of gospel witness, believers often encounter significant challenges when attempting to share their faith. Understanding these barriers is critical to preparing effectively and persevering with courage and wisdom.

---

[111] Craig S. Keener, *Acts: An Exegetical Commentary*, vol. 2 (Grand Rapids, MI: Baker Academic, 2013), 1544

One of the most pervasive challenges is fear—fear of rejection, misunderstanding, or damaging relationships. The cultural stigma surrounding religious discussions, particularly those involving claims to absolute truth, often deters believers from initiating gospel conversations. However, as theologian Timothy Keller reminds us, "The gospel is offensive because it confronts our pride, but we must never be offensive in how we communicate it."[112] Believers are called to share the truth with gentleness and respect, even when rejection is a possibility (1 Pet. 3:15).

Cultural relativism presents another formidable obstacle. In a postmodern society that prizes individual autonomy and subjective truth, the exclusive claims of Christianity are frequently met with skepticism or hostility. David Wells notes, "In a world where the self is sovereign, the idea of a transcendent, moral God is deeply offensive."[113] Believers must learn to articulate the uniqueness of Christ with humility and clarity, avoiding triumphalism while faithfully upholding biblical truth (John 14:6).

A third challenge is the perceived inadequacy or lack of preparation among many believers. Some feel ill-equipped to share their faith effectively, fearing they lack sufficient theological knowledge or rhetorical skill. However, as William Lane Craig emphasizes, "The most effective apologetic is often a life that demonstrates the reality of God's love and grace."[114]

---

[112] Timothy Keller, *Center Church: Doing Balanced, Gospel-Centered Ministry in Your City* (Grand Rapids, MI: Zondervan, 2012), 221

[113] David F. Wells, *God in the Whirlwind: How the Holy-love of God Reorients Our World* (Wheaton, IL: Crossway, 2014), 56

[114] William Lane Craig, *On Guard: Defending Your Faith with Reason and Precision* (Colorado Springs, CO: David C. Cook, 2010), 35

Personal testimony, rooted in an authentic relationship with Christ, remains one of the most powerful forms of gospel witness (John 4:39).

Furthermore, the relentless pace of modern life and the distractions of technology often breed spiritual complacency, diminishing the urgency of gospel witness. Os Guinness warns, "Never has a society been more distracted, and never has distraction been more dangerous for the people of God."[115] Intentional spiritual disciplines such as prayer, Scripture study, and regular reflection are essential to maintaining a Kingdom-focused perspective and overcoming apathy.

Finally, spiritual opposition must not be underestimated. Scripture affirms that gospel witness unfolds within the context of spiritual warfare (Eph. 6:12). Evangelistic efforts are often met with discouragement, resistance, or subtle deception intended to undermine boldness. John Stott observes, "The devil's primary strategy is to silence the Church."[116] Believers must remain vigilant, clothed in spiritual armor, and dependent on the Holy Spirit's empowering presence (Eph. 6:13-18).

By recognizing these common challenges—fear, cultural relativism, inadequacy, complacency, and spiritual opposition—believers are better positioned to address them with biblical wisdom and courageous faith. In doing so, they remain faithful to Christ's commission to shine and share the gospel in a world desperately needing His redeeming grace.

---

[115] Os Guinness, *Fool's Talk: Recovering the Art of Christian Persuasion* (Downers Grove, IL: IVP Books, 2015), 112
[116] John Stott, *The Message of Ephesians* (Downers Grove, IL: InterVarsity Press, 1979), 260

Practical Strategies for Effective Witness

For believers to shine as Kingdom witnesses, gospel proclamation must be accompanied by intentional, Spirit-led strategies that reflect both biblical wisdom and cultural sensitivity. Effective witness is not haphazard; it requires preparation, authenticity, and dependence on God's power.

First, relational evangelism remains indispensable. Building authentic, trust-based relationships opens doors for gospel conversations that are rooted in love rather than obligation. As missiologist Michael Frost notes, "People are drawn to Jesus when they encounter His presence embodied in loving, gracious relationships."[117] This approach requires patience, empathy, and a willingness to walk alongside others in their spiritual journey.

Second, contextualization is vital. Gospel truth never changes, but how it is communicated must account for cultural, social, and personal factors. Paul modeled this approach by becoming "all things to all people" so that he might win some (1 Cor. 9:22). Andrew Walls emphasizes that "Christianity is always both universal and particular—adaptable to diverse cultures while remaining anchored in apostolic truth."[118] An effective witness speaks the language of the hearer's heart without diluting the gospel.

Third, spiritual preparation through prayer and dependence on the Holy Spirit is essential. Gospel witness is

---

[117] Michael Frost, *Surprise the World: The Five Habits of Highly Missional People* (Colorado Springs, CO: NavPress, 2016), 57
[118] Andrew F. Walls, *The Missionary Movement in Christian History: Studies in the Transmission of Faith* (Maryknoll, NY: Orbis Books, 1996), 15

ultimately a spiritual endeavor requiring divine empowerment. Jesus commanded His disciples to wait for the Spirit's empowerment before beginning their mission (Acts 1:8). As J. I. Packer reminds us, "Evangelism is not ultimately human persuasion but divine regeneration."[119] Spirit-led boldness and discernment are key to fruitful witness.

Additionally, equipping oneself with biblical knowledge and apologetic training builds confidence and competence. As Greg Koukl asserts, "We are called to be ambassadors for Christ—gracious, knowledgeable, and wise in our interactions."[120] Training enables believers to articulate the gospel clearly, answer common objections, and engage in meaningful dialogue with skeptics.

Moreover, personal testimony remains a powerful tool. Sharing one's authentic experience of encountering Christ often resonates more deeply than abstract theological arguments. Testimony combines vulnerability and hope, revealing the tangible impact of the gospel on real lives. As evangelist Rebecca Pippert observes, "Evangelism is simply joining the conversation God is already having with someone."[121]

Finally, participating in a supportive Christian community fosters ongoing encouragement, accountability, and collective witness. The early church's vibrant community life

---

[119] J. I. Packer, *Evangelism and the Sovereignty of God* (Downers Grove, IL: IVP, 1961), 27

[120] Greg Koukl, *Tactics: A Game Plan for Discussing Your Christian Convictions* (Grand Rapids, MI: Zondervan, 2009), 41

[121] Rebecca Manley Pippert, *Out of the Saltshaker and into the World: Evangelism as a Way of Life* (Downers Grove, IL: IVP, 1999), 23

(Acts 2:42-47) demonstrated how love, service, and unity create an environment where the gospel flourishes.

By embracing these strategies—relational evangelism, contextualization, spiritual preparation, training, authentic testimony, and community support—believers position themselves to share the gospel effectively, demonstrating both the truth and beauty of life in Christ.

Conclusion: Living as Effective Kingdom Witnesses

Living as Kingdom witnesses involves intentionality and spiritual sensitivity, requiring believers to integrate gospel-sharing into every facet of their daily lives. Effective witnessing goes beyond merely speaking the gospel message; it requires consistently embodying Christ's character and compassion. As Christopher J. H. Wright contends, "Our lives are meant to be visible demonstrations of God's mission, not merely vehicles for religious words."[122] Believers who authentically reflect Christ through their lives, attitudes, and interactions create compelling testimonies that naturally draw others toward Him.

As ambassadors for Christ, Christians are called to a life characterized by integrity, humility, and unwavering commitment to the truth. They must courageously navigate cultural challenges, overcome personal fears, and actively seek meaningful opportunities to engage with others. As Michael Green explains, "Evangelism is not an isolated act but a lifestyle that flows from deep intimacy with God."[123] Spiritual disciplines

---

[122] Christopher J. H. Wright, *The Mission of God's People: A Biblical Theology of the Church's Mission* (Grand Rapids, MI: Zondervan, 2010), 215.
[123] Michael Green, *Evangelism in the Early Church* (Grand Rapids, MI: Eerdmans, 2004), 12

such as prayer, Scripture study, and fellowship within the community of faith fortify believers spiritually and practically for effective witness.

Ultimately, the call to shine and share the gospel is a profound privilege and a sacred responsibility. Believers who respond faithfully to this call will witness the transformative power of the gospel impacting individuals and communities, advancing God's Kingdom in remarkable and lasting ways. As believers step forward boldly in their mission, they faithfully live out the Great Commission, bringing glory to God and hope to a world in need of Christ.

Chapter 15

Live with a Kingdom Vision: Seeing Life Through God's Eternal Perspective

To live with a Kingdom vision is to see the world through God's eternal perspective, where every moment, action, and decision is situated within His redemptive plan. This vision is not merely an inspirational ideal but a deeply transformative framework that shapes a believer's understanding of purpose, identity, and destiny. Scripture consistently urges believers to set their minds on eternal realities: "Set your minds on things that are above, not on things that are on earth" (Col. 3:2). Without this perspective, Christians risk falling into the insidious patterns of a culture fixated on immediacy, materialism, and self-fulfillment. With it, they are liberated to live with wisdom, sacrificial love, and enduring hope.

The dangers of neglecting this eternal perspective are manifold and pervasive in contemporary society. A culture fixated on immediacy compels individuals to seek instant gratification, leading to short-sighted decisions in finances, relationships, and spiritual growth. The relentless pursuit of material possessions, often fueled by advertising and social comparison, can ensnare believers in a cycle of discontent and endless craving, diverting their affections from eternal treasures. Furthermore, the modern emphasis on self-fulfillment, while not inherently wrong, can subtly shift focus from God's glory to personal ambition, fostering a subtle narcissism that undermines the selfless call of Christ. In such an environment, the Christian risks becoming indistinguishable from the world, their faith reduced to a mere add-on to an otherwise secular life rather than the transformative core of their being. This drift away from eternal priorities can result in a superficial faith, easily swayed by trends and trials, lacking the deep roots necessary for steadfastness.

John Calvin describes this orientation as the heart being "raised above this world to set its affections on the hope of immortality," recognizing that all earthly endeavors are fleeting apart from God's eternal purposes.[124] This eternal focus reframes how believers view suffering, success, relationships, and vocation—not as endpoints but as part of God's grand narrative. Success, for example, is no longer solely measured by earthly metrics of wealth or status, but by faithfulness and glorifying God. Suffering is not a meaningless aberration but a crucible for refining character and deepening trust in God's sovereign plan (Romans 8:28).

N. T. Wright explains, "The church is not simply a collection of individuals with their own private salvation, but a body called to anticipate God's new creation in its life together."[125] In this light, living with Kingdom vision becomes an individual and communal calling, compelling believers to reflect God's character in every sphere of life. This framework

---

[124] John Calvin, *Institutes of the Christian Religion*, trans. Henry Beveridge (Peabody, MA: Hendrickson, 2008), III.25
[125] N. T. Wright, *After You Believe: Why Christian Character Matters* (New York: HarperOne, 2010), 115

transcends mere intellectual assent; it transforms priorities, shapes daily choices, and informs reactions to adversity, ultimately guiding believers toward a life that truly counts. As Psalm 90:12 implores, "Teach us to number our days, that we may gain a heart of wisdom," highlighting the direct link between an awareness of life's brevity and cultivating an eternal mindset. Similarly, Jesus' teaching in Matthew 6:19-21 to "store up for yourselves treasures in heaven" serves as a direct counter-cultural command, challenging the impulse to accumulate earthly wealth and instead orienting our efforts towards what truly lasts.

Furthermore, a Kingdom vision offers profound resilience amid trials and uncertainties. Jürgen Moltmann notes, "Hope alone is to be called 'realistic,' because it takes seriously the possibilities with which all reality is fraught."[126] Biblical hope is not passive optimism but active anticipation, a dynamic force that reshapes the present in light of God's promised future. This perspective guards against despair and complacency, fostering instead a life marked by joyful expectation, courageous action, and steadfast faith. A Kingdom vision allows believers to see beyond the immediate pain to God's overarching purposes when faced with economic downturns, relational breakdowns, or personal health crises. It cultivates a deep-seated peace that is not dependent on circumstances, but on the unshakeable character of God and the certainty of His ultimate triumph.

This chapter will explore how a Kingdom vision redefines reality, how Jesus models this vision, and how believers today are invited to embody it. We will trace the

---

[126] Jürgen Moltmann, *Theology of Hope* (Minneapolis, MN: Fortress Press, 1993), 23

theological foundations, practical implications, and enduring impact of seeing life through God's eternal lens—ultimately showing that living with a Kingdom vision aligns one's heart with the heartbeat of God's unfolding story. This journey will invite us to consider how such a perspective can empower us to live lives of profound meaning, unwavering purpose, and lasting significance in a world often distracted by the transient.

The God-Centered Lens: Reframing Reality

A Kingdom vision reframes the believer's reality by shifting the central focus from the self to God. Scripture calls believers to orient every part of life toward God's purposes in a world where personal ambition, success, and fulfillment are often treated as ultimate goals. Miroslav Volf writes, "To live under the reign of God is to live with a reality that transcends our own small stories and places them into God's greater drama of redemption."[127] This means interpreting joys, losses, work, and suffering through the framework of divine sovereignty (Rom. 8:28). This God-centered lens transforms how we experience and respond to life's myriad experiences.

Consider how this reframing applies to joys and successes. Instead of taking sole credit for accomplishments, a Kingdom-minded believer recognizes God as the ultimate source of all gifts and opportunities. This perspective fosters deep gratitude, not pride. When a project succeeds, a promotion is gained, or a personal goal is achieved, the focus shifts from self-congratulation to acknowledging God's grace and sovereignty. It prevents the trap of idolatry, where our achievements become

---

[127] Miroslav Volf, *A Public Faith: How Followers of Christ Should Serve the Common Good* (Grand Rapids, MI: Brazos Press, 2011), 65

sources of ultimate identity or security, and instead directs all glory back to the Giver. This reorientation enables joyful celebration without falling into arrogance, knowing that true success lies in honoring God.

Conversely, a God-centered lens provides profound meaning in losses and suffering. In a world that often seeks to avoid pain at all costs, the believer understands that hardship can be a refining fire, a means by which God purifies character, deepens faith, and draws His children closer to Himself. While pain is real and should be acknowledged, it is not seen as meaningless or arbitrary. Romans 8:28, often quoted, truly comes alive through this lens: "And we know that in all things God works for the good of those who love him, who have been called according to his purpose." This does not mean suffering is good in itself, but that God is able to redeem it and use it for ultimate good—often for spiritual formation or for the advance of His Kingdom. This perspective fuels resilience, enabling believers to endure with hope, knowing God is present and at work even in the darkest valleys. Teresa of Avila's timeless wisdom reminds believers, "Let nothing disturb you... God never changes. Patience obtains all things." Such God-centeredness moves believers away from temporal anxieties and toward spiritual stability and hope, providing an unshakeable anchor in life's storms.

Furthermore, this lens redefines work and vocation. For the Kingdom-minded, work is not merely a means to a paycheck or personal advancement, but a sphere of divine appointment. Whether in the boardroom, the classroom, the hospital, or the home, every task can be elevated into an act of worship and service to God. Professionals in any field can ask: How can I bring God's truth, justice, and excellence into my work? How can my daily tasks reflect His character and contribute to human flourishing? This understanding imbues even the most mundane duties with profound purpose, transforming a mere job into a calling, and enabling believers to see their professional lives as integral parts of God's redemptive plan for the world.

Significantly, a God-centered lens profoundly affects ethical and relational choices. When believers view themselves not as owners but as stewards of their resources, time, talents, and even their very lives, they are liberated from the grip of greed and self-preservation. This stewardship mindset compels generosity, integrity, and responsible living. Possessions are seen as tools for Kingdom advance, not ends in themselves. Similarly, when others are viewed not as competitors, instruments for personal gain, or mere acquaintances, but as fellow image-bearers of God, relationships are transformed. This recognition demands respect, empathy, and a commitment to justice, mercy, and humility (Mic. 6:8). The early church provides a powerful example of this radical reorientation, where "all the believers were one in heart and mind. No one claimed that any of their possessions was their own, but they shared everything they had" (Acts 4:32). Their practices of radical generosity and hospitality (Acts 2:42–47) were direct outflows of their God-centered perspective, demonstrating a counter-cultural community living out Kingdom values. As Rowan Williams observes, "The Christian vision of humanity is one in which every face carries the imprint of Christ."[128] To embrace this lens is to embrace a comprehensive reorientation of life, values, and mission,

---

[128] Rowan Williams, *Being Christian* (Grand Rapids, MI: Eerdmans, 2014), 45

profoundly impacting how we interact with the world around us. This reorientation prompts critical questions: What truly holds my loyalty? Do my daily choices reflect God's priorities or the world's? Am I living as a consumer or a contributor to God's Kingdom?

Jesus, the Perfect Vision-Carrier

Jesus Christ is the supreme example of Kingdom vision, embodying unwavering alignment with the Father's will throughout His earthly ministry. From His baptism to His final moments on the cross, Jesus revealed a life directed not by human ambition but by divine mission. As N. T. Wright explains, "Jesus' life was a continual enacting of God's future in the present, pulling the reality of God's kingdom into the midst of human history."[129] His teachings, miracles, and interactions were all infused with a perspective that reached beyond earthly concerns to the eternal purposes of God.

Jesus' Kingdom vision profoundly shaped how He saw people, especially the marginalized—the poor, the sick, the sinners, and the outcasts. In a society that often ostracized these groups, Jesus actively sought them out. He touched the leper, dined with tax collectors, and offered forgiveness to prostitutes. His compassion was not a mere sentiment but a concrete demonstration of the Kingdom breaking into the world, bringing healing, restoration, and dignity to those society had deemed unworthy. Each act of healing, word of forgiveness, and inclusion of an outcast was a tangible manifestation of God's reign, signaling that the divine order was one of mercy and

---

[129] N. T. Wright, *After You Believe: Why Christian Character Matters* (New York: HarperOne, 2010), 115

justice, fundamentally challenging His day's prevailing social and religious norms. His parables, such as the Good Samaritan, the Prodigal Son, and the Lost Sheep, eloquently articulated God's heart for the lost and marginalized, urging His followers to adopt the same inclusive, redemptive posture.

Dietrich Bonhoeffer poignantly writes, "When Christ calls a man, he bids him come and die," highlighting that following Jesus is surrendering self-centeredness in favor of costly discipleship.[130] This "death" is not merely physical but a death to one's own desires, ambitions, and ego, surrendering them to Christ's Lordship. For Jesus, costly discipleship meant rejection, misunderstanding, and crucifixion. For believers today, it can mean prioritizing the Kingdom over career advancement, sacrificing personal comfort for the sake of justice, or choosing forgiveness over retaliation. It challenges the notion that faith is a pathway to an easy life, revealing that authentic discipleship involves a willingness to embrace suffering and sacrifice for God's greater purposes.

The Garden of Gethsemane is a pivotal illustration of Jesus' Kingdom-centered living. His anguished yet faithful prayer — "Not my will, but yours be done" (Luke 22:42) — encapsulates the essence of this surrender. Here, Jesus faced the crushing weight of the cross, the ultimate sacrifice, yet His unwavering focus on the Father's redemptive plan allowed Him to choose obedience. Even under extreme pressure, with the full weight of human sin about to be laid upon Him, Jesus entrusted Himself to the Father's plan, modeling resilience, courage, and a love that would ultimately triumph over death. His struggle was

---

[130] Dietrich Bonhoeffer, *The Cost of Discipleship* (New York: Macmillan, 1959), 44

real, human, yet His ultimate resolve was divine. This example empowers believers to confront their own "Gethsemane moments"—those times of intense trial, fear, or difficult choices—with a similar trust and commitment to God's will, knowing that true victory comes through obedience and surrender. As Hebrews 12:2 affirms, "For the joy set before Him, He endured the cross, scorning its shame, and sat down at the right hand of the throne of God." Jesus' unwavering focus on God's mission challenges believers today to adopt a similar eternal perspective, reshaping how they approach sacrifice, leadership, and witness, knowing that present suffering holds eternal weight and future glory. His life unequivocally demonstrated that true leadership is servant leadership, true power is found in humility, and faithful witness is found in living a life that perfectly reflects the Father's heart.

The Transforming Power of Hope

Hope is the driving force behind a Kingdom vision. Unlike secular optimism, which is often based on favorable circumstances or positive thinking, biblical hope is anchored in the steadfast promises of God and the unshakeable assurance of His redemptive work. Paul writes, "For in this hope we were saved. But hope that is seen is no hope at all" (Rom. 8:24), pointing believers beyond immediate circumstances toward the certain fulfillment of God's purposes. This distinction is crucial: secular optimism is fragile, easily shattered by adverse events, whereas biblical hope is robust, able to withstand the fiercest storms because its foundation is not human capability or worldly conditions, but the unchanging character and faithfulness of God Himself.

Jürgen Moltmann observes, "Hope draws the future into the present, transforming it and reshaping it in accordance with the promises of God."[131] This understanding of hope does not ignore suffering or gloss over pain; rather, it interprets it within God's greater story of renewal and redemption. It allows believers to acknowledge the brokenness of the present world while simultaneously living in the light of the future Kingdom that is undoubtedly coming. This active, transformative hope inspires action, propelling believers to live out the values of the Kingdom now, even when the full realization of God's promises seems distant. It provides the courage to persevere, the motivation to serve, and the strength to believe that their labor in the Lord is never in vain.

Throughout history, Christians have drawn immense strength from this hope in times of brutal persecution, agonizing exile, and profound hardship. The early martyrs, facing torturous deaths in Roman arenas, often went to their demise with hymns on their lips, not because they were naive to their suffering, but because they were profoundly convinced of the resurrection and God's faithfulness. Their hope transcended their present pain, rooted in the certainty of eternal life and vindication in Christ. Centuries later, during the horrors of the Holocaust, individuals like Corrie ten Boom, who survived a Nazi concentration camp, bore witness to this enduring hope. She famously reflected, "There is no pit so deep that God's love is not deeper still."[132] Her testimony, born from unimaginable suffering, demonstrates how biblical hope can empower forgiveness, foster resilience,

---

[131] Jürgen Moltmann, *Theology of Hope* (Minneapolis, MN: Fortress Press, 1993), 35

[132] Corrie ten Boom, *The Hiding Place* (Grand Rapids, MI: Chosen Books, 1971), 217

and fuel joyful obedience even in the face of absolute evil. This transformative hope fosters resilience, empowers forgiveness, and fuels joyful obedience. It equips believers to resist despair, to endure with perseverance, and to live as heralds of the coming Kingdom, offering light in the darkest places.

Biblical hope is not escapism; it is a force that anchors believers firmly in the present while orienting them toward eternity. As Hebrews 6:19 says, "We have this hope as an anchor for the soul, firm and secure." This anchor prevents believers from being tossed about by changing circumstances or waves of cultural anxiety. Such hope profoundly reshapes daily living, calling believers to embody faithfulness even when uncertain or seemingly hopeless circumstances exist. It transforms how Christians navigate grief, loss, and disappointment—not by minimizing pain or denying sorrow, but by locating it within God's larger, redemptive restoration narrative. This means that while tears may fall, they fall in the light of a promise that all things will be made new, that every tear will be wiped away, and that ultimate justice and joy will prevail. This hope provides comfort and a profound sense of purpose, empowering believers to live proactively, knowing that their present actions contribute to an eternal reality. It inspires prayer, patience, and persistent good works, all flowing from the conviction that God is faithful to His promises and His Kingdom will ultimately come in its fullness.

Pilgrims and Ambassadors: Our Dual Identity

Living with a Kingdom vision calls believers to embrace a profound dual identity: we are both pilgrims journeying through a world that is not our ultimate home and ambassadors representing the reign of God within it. This inherent tension defines much of the Christian experience and shapes how believers ought to engage with the world.

The letter to the Hebrews describes the faithful as "strangers and exiles on the earth" (Heb. 11:13), recognizing that ultimate belonging lies not in earthly systems, nations, or cultures, but in the City of God. This pilgrim identity has profound implications for how believers relate to material possessions, career success, and social status. It fosters a healthy detachment from temporal idols, reminding us that nothing on earth can offer ultimate security or lasting satisfaction. This perspective encourages generosity and simplicity, as earthly wealth is seen as a means to advance the Kingdom, not an end in itself. It cultivates a sense of gratitude for temporary blessings while preventing over-reliance on them. The pilgrim mindset keeps believers from becoming too comfortable in the world, lest they forget their proper destination. It calls for a constant orientation toward eternal promises, reminding us that our true "home" is with God. This detachment allows freedom from the relentless pursuit of more, the fear of losing what we have, and the constant striving for worldly recognition. It redefines "home" not as a physical location, but as a spiritual dwelling in God's presence.

However, Christians are not merely waiting passively for heaven; they are sent into the world as **ambassadors of Christ** (2 Cor. 5:20), tasked with embodying and proclaiming the values of God's Kingdom here and now. Lesslie Newbigin explains, "The church is the sign, instrument, and foretaste of the kingdom of God,"[133] meaning that believers are called to be visible

---

[133] Lesslie Newbigin, *The Gospel in a Pluralist Society* (Grand Rapids, MI: Eerdmans, 1989), 110

witnesses of God's redemptive work in their communities and cultures. Believers carry a weighty responsibility as ambassadors: faithfully representing Christ and His Kingdom to a watching world. This involves living out the Kingdom values of justice, mercy, truth, righteousness, peace, and sacrificial love in every sphere of life. It means being agents of reconciliation in a divided world, advocates for the oppressed, and bearers of truth in a culture often confused by relativism. This dual identity—of being both not fully at home and yet fully engaged—defines the Christian life. It demands navigating the tension of being "in the world but not of the world" (John 17:14-16), a delicate balance that requires deep spiritual discernment.

This dual identity has historically shaped the church's most profound societal contributions. From the tireless efforts of William Wilberforce and other abolitionists who fought against the transatlantic slave trade, driven by a conviction of human dignity rooted in God's image, to the unwavering compassion of figures like Dorothy Day, who championed the rights and dignity of the poor and marginalized through the Catholic Worker Movement, Christians have labored not as cultural conformists or separatists but as Kingdom ambassadors. They have actively sought justice, mercy, and reconciliation in Christ's name, demonstrating that faith is not a private affair but a public calling. As Augustine taught in *The City of God*, believers live within two cities—the City of Man and the City of God—and are called to serve the former while ultimately belonging to the latter.[134] This means actively participating in civil society, seeking the common good, and influencing culture with Kingdom principles while

---

[134] Augustine, *The City of God*, trans. Henry Bettenson (London: Penguin Classics, 2003), XIX.17

remembering that their ultimate allegiance and hope lie beyond earthly realms.

To live as pilgrims and ambassadors is to walk in both humility and authority: humility stemming from the recognition that this world is not our ultimate home and all we have is from God; authority derived from being representatives of the King of Kings. It demands that believers carry the world's burdens—its brokenness, suffering, and injustices—while simultaneously offering it the transformative hope of Christ. It requires discernment to know when to engage, when to challenge, and when to withdraw. It calls for courage to stand for truth in a relativistic age and unwavering faith that God's Kingdom will ultimately prevail. This identity anchors believers in the truth that their citizenship is in heaven (Phil. 3:20) even as they work for the good of the world they inhabit, shaping it with eternal values. It is a call to proactive engagement, not passive waiting; a dynamic tension that fuels our longing for heaven and our labor for its realization on earth.

Cultural Discernment: Engaging Without Compromising

Living with a Kingdom vision also requires profound cultural discernment, which is engaging the world wisely without compromising the distinctiveness of the Christian faith. Jesus described His followers as being "in the world but not of the world" (John 17:14–16), a tension that calls for thoughtful, faithful presence in society. This means Christians are not to retreat into isolated enclaves, nor are they to uncritically assimilate into every cultural trend. Instead, they are called to a dynamic engagement, acting as salt and light (Matthew 5:13-16), preserving what is good and illuminating truth in the surrounding darkness. James Davison Hunter articulates this challenge as a call to "faithful presence," which means participating fully in the spheres of culture — work, politics, art, education, entertainment, family — while bearing witness to God's truth and grace.[135]

Cultural discernment involves both affirmation and critique. Believers are called to recognize the goodness of creation, the inherent value of human creativity, and the potential for good within social institutions. Art, music, scientific discovery, and acts of civic kindness can all, in various ways, reflect aspects of God's character and His design for flourishing. Christians can appreciate and celebrate these elements, acknowledging them as common grace. However, discernment also necessitates **resisting cultural currents that distort God's design**. This includes ideologies that promote materialism, injustice, moral relativism, or the worship of self. For example, while technology can be a powerful tool for good, cultural discernment would critique its potential for fostering isolation, promoting instant gratification, or spreading misinformation. While financial success is not inherently evil, a Kingdom vision would critique a culture that defines human worth solely by wealth or encourages ruthless competition at the expense of ethical conduct. Tim Keller explains that Christians should be "a counterculture for the common good," reflecting values that challenge idols of power, wealth, and self-interest, offering a compelling alternative rooted in God's truth and love.[136] They

---

[135] James Davison Hunter, *To Change the World: The Irony, Tragedy, and Possibility of Christianity in the Late Modern World* (New York: Oxford University Press, 2010), 243
[136] Timothy Keller, *Center Church: Doing Balanced, Gospel-Centered Ministry in Your City* (Grand Rapids, MI: Zondervan, 2012), 290

are called to be distinct not for distinctness' sake, but for the sake of offering a more beautiful, just, and life-giving way of being.

Cultural discernment requires ongoing **wisdom, humility, and dependence on the Holy Spirit**. It means diligently studying Scripture, prayerfully seeking God's guidance, and engaging in robust community with other believers to gain varied perspectives. It involves knowing when to stand firm on non-negotiable truths, when to build bridges of understanding and dialogue, and when to offer constructive critique from a place of love. It means engaging with media, art, and political discourse not as passive consumers, but as active participants seeking to understand and respond in ways that honor God. Ultimately, it reflects a heart deeply committed to God's truth and a life willing to serve the world without losing its soul (Mark 8:36). This discernment is not merely an intellectual exercise but a spiritual discipline, enabling believers to navigate complex contemporary issues with clarity, courage, and compassion, always aiming to point others towards the light of the Kingdom.

Shaping Legacy and Impact

A Kingdom vision reshapes how believers live today and the enduring legacy they leave behind. Rather than measuring success by fleeting metrics such as wealth accumulated, titles held, or personal achievements celebrated, a Kingdom-centered legacy is marked by faithfulness, sacrificial love, and the transformative impact made in the lives of others. The focus shifts from temporary accomplishments, which fade with time, to eternal investments — nurturing relationships, discipling others, serving the poor and vulnerable, and faithfully contributing to God's ongoing redemptive work in the world.

This understanding of legacy fundamentally reorients priorities. **Purposeful living** leads directly to **purposeful influence**. When believers align their time, talents, financial resources, and spiritual gifts with God's purposes, they become powerful conduits of His grace and transformation. This legacy is not confined to public ministry or large platforms; often, the quiet, consistent acts of love and faith bear the most lasting fruit. Consider the countless unsung heroes of faith: the parent who faithfully raises children in the discipline and instruction of the Lord, instilling biblical values that ripple through generations; the friend who consistently encourages a struggling peer, offering a listening ear and prayer; the mentor who pours into younger believers, equipping them for future service; the volunteer who faithfully serves in a local church, contributing to the spiritual formation of their community; or the neighbor who consistently extends kindness and hospitality, creating pockets of Kingdom presence on their street. These seemingly small acts, born of a Kingdom vision, are profound, eternal investments, accumulating spiritual dividends that far outweigh any earthly recognition. They reflect God's heart and leave an indelible mark on individuals and communities.

Importantly, shaping a Kingdom-minded legacy requires profound **intentionality**. It calls believers to regularly reflect on how they steward the gifts and opportunities God has entrusted to them. It demands asking hard questions about one's priorities and investments: What story will my life tell at its end? Am I building something that will last, or merely accumulating fleeting comforts? What eternal mark am I leaving on the lives of those around me? This intentionality involves prayerful discernment about vocational choices, financial decisions, and allocating one's most precious resource: time. It means actively seeking opportunities to serve, to share the gospel, to advocate for justice, and to invest in relationships that foster spiritual growth. Living with the "end in mind" — the ultimate reality of God's Kingdom — shapes every present choice, ensuring that actions taken today contribute to a lasting, eternal impact.

Scripture profoundly reminds believers that their labor in the Lord is never in vain (1 Cor. 15:58). This promise is a powerful encouragement, assuring them that even small acts of faithfulness, hidden deeds of kindness, or unseen prayers carry immeasurable eternal significance. It liberates believers from the pressure of seeking human applause and anchors their efforts in God's approval. To live with a Kingdom vision is to live beyond oneself — to sow seeds of truth, love, and righteousness that will flourish long after one's earthly life is done. It is an invitation to become an active, vital part of God's ongoing story of redemption, leaving behind a trail of hope, faith, and love that points future generations, and indeed the whole world, to Christ and His coming Kingdom. This legacy is not etched in stone monuments, but in transformed lives and a world slowly, yet surely, being conformed to the image of its Creator.

Conclusion: Fixing Our Eyes on the Unseen

To live with a Kingdom vision is to fix our eyes on the unseen realities of God's Kingdom, allowing those eternal truths to shape our everyday decisions, relationships, and aspirations. This perspective invites believers to walk by faith, not by sight, anchoring their lives in the steadfast promises of God even when circumstances seem uncertain, challenging, or overwhelmingly bleak. As the apostle Paul writes, "For our light and momentary troubles are achieving for us an eternal glory that far outweighs them all" (2 Cor. 4:17). With such an outlook, trials are no longer viewed as pointless suffering but become refining tools, meticulously shaped by God's hand to produce endurance, character, and hope. Successes transform from opportunities for self-congratulation into moments of profound gratitude and opportunities to give glory back to God. Ordinary moments become sacred encounters, imbued with purpose and significance when viewed through the lens of God's unfolding story. This profound shift in perspective transforms the mundane into the meaningful, the painful into the purposeful.

This vision is not a call to escape the world or withdraw from its complexities but to engage it with renewed purpose and divine strategy. It equips believers to live boldly yet humbly, to serve generously yet wisely, and to lead lives marked by unwavering faith, resilient hope, and self-sacrificing love. Significantly, it fundamentally shifts the focus from temporal gain—financial prosperity, social status, or fleeting pleasures—to eternal significance. This shift helps Christians to courageously resist pervasive cultural pressures that define human worth by achievement, material possession, or public reputation. It liberates them from the exhausting race for more, offering instead the deep satisfaction of living for something truly lasting.

Living with a Kingdom vision ultimately aligns one's heart and mind. It will be with God's grand narrative of redemption, a narrative that began in creation, was interrupted by the fall, redeemed by Christ, and will culminate in the new heavens and new earth. It is a clarion call to be faithful stewards of all God has entrusted to us, understanding that everything belongs to Him. It is a commission to be resilient pilgrims, navigating this earthly journey with our eyes fixed on our heavenly destination. Moreover, it is an urgent mandate to be courageous ambassadors, representing Christ and bearing witness to God's love, justice, and truth in a broken world that desperately needs to see and experience His Kingdom.

As believers consistently fix their eyes on Jesus—the author and perfecter of our faith, the very embodiment of the Kingdom vision—they are strengthened to persevere through every obstacle, empowered by His Spirit to serve others sacrificially, and commissioned to shine as lights pointing others toward the hope of the gospel. In doing so, they not only honor God with their lives, transforming their earthly existence into an act of worship, but they also actively participate in His ongoing work, preparing themselves and countless others for the unsurpassed joy and eternal glory of His coming Kingdom, where His reign will be fully established, and every tear will be wiped away. This is every believer's ultimate vision, hope, and purpose: to live now in light of that glorious future.

Chapter 16

The Trinity and the Relational Nature of God: Implications for Humanity

Among the most profound and beautiful truths of the Christian faith is the doctrine of the Trinity — the confession that God is one in essence and three in persons: Father, Son, and Holy Spirit. This is not a dry theological concept but the heartbeat of Christian life and worship. To encounter the Triune God is to be drawn into the eternal communion of love that existed before the world's foundation. As theologian Michael Reeves writes, "The Christian life is knowing God as Father, enjoying the Son, and being enlivened by the Spirit."[137]

The Trinity is not merely an abstract formula but the living reality that shapes all of creation, redemption, and human existence. It reveals that at the core of all things is not isolation or power but relationship and love. When Jesus prays in John 17:24, "Father, I desire that they also, whom you have given me, may be with me where I am," He draws His followers into the eternal fellowship of the Godhead. This means that Christian life is about believing certain doctrines or following moral

---

[137] Michael Reeves, *Delighting in the Trinity* (Downers Grove, IL: InterVarsity Press, 2012), 26.

commands and communion with God, who is Himself communion.

This chapter will explore how the doctrine of the Trinity unfolds in Scripture, how it was clarified in Christian history, and how it shapes human identity and community today. We will reflect on what it means to be made in the image of a relational God and how the Triune nature of God invites us into a life of love, unity, and mission. Far from being an intellectual exercise, the Trinity is the foundation for worship, relationships, and the church's witness to the world.

The Biblical Revelation of the Trinity

The doctrine of the Trinity, while never formally articulated under that name in Scripture, is revealed progressively through the biblical narrative. The Old Testament offers hints of God's triune nature, such as in Genesis 1:26, where God says, "Let us make man in our image, after our likeness," suggesting plurality within the divine unity. Similarly, the Spirit of God is depicted as active in creation (Gen. 1:2) and in empowering leaders, prophets, and kings (Judg. 3:10; Isa. 61:1). While the fullness of the Trinity remains veiled in the Old Testament, these anticipatory glimpses prepare the way for its clearer unveiling in Christ.

In the New Testament, the Trinity shines forth unmistakably. At Jesus' baptism, we see Father, Son, and Spirit simultaneously at work: the Father's voice declares, "This is my beloved Son," while the Spirit descends like a dove upon Jesus (Matt. 3:16–17). Jesus' own teachings affirm His unique relationship with the Father, as when He declares, "I and the Father are one" (John 10:30), or when He promises the coming of the Helper, the Holy Spirit, who proceeds from the Father (John 14:26). The Great Commission (Matt. 28:19) calls the church to baptize disciples "in the name of the Father and of the Son and of the Holy Spirit," offering a profoundly Trinitarian framework for mission and identity.

The Apostle Paul regularly anchors his letters in Trinitarian patterns, blessing churches with "the grace of the Lord Jesus Christ, and the love of God, and the fellowship of the Holy Spirit" (2 Cor. 13:14). The Book of Revelation offers a doxological climax, presenting the Lamb, the One seated on the throne, and the sevenfold Spirit in harmonious worship (Rev. 5:6–13). Scripture reveals a God who is both one and three, a unity-in-diversity that becomes the heartbeat of Christian theology, worship, and life.

Theological Foundations: One Essence, Three Persons

The theological foundation of the Trinity rests on the conviction that God is one in essence and three in persons — Father, Son, and Holy Spirit. This foundational truth safeguards Christian faith against two significant errors: tritheism (the belief in three gods) and modalism (the belief that God is one person who manifests in different modes). The Nicene Creed (AD 325), one of the church's most enduring confessions, affirms that the Son is "begotten, not made, being of one substance with the Father," and that the Spirit "proceeds from the Father and the Son," highlighting both the unity and distinction within the Godhead.

William Burt Pope emphasized that "every word [must be] faithful to the equal honour of each of the Three Adorable Persons in the unity of the Other Two, and in the unity of the

Godhead."[138] This sacred unity is not one of mere agreement but of shared essence and intentional relational interdependence. The Father loves the Son and glorifies Him (John 17:1–5); the Son submits to the will of the Father (John 6:38); and the Spirit proceeds from both the Father and the Son (John 15:26). As Augustus Hopkins Strong explains, there is a "single essence manifesting in three persons who are in constant, divine fellowship."[139]

Early church theologians like Athanasius and the Cappadocian Fathers labored to clarify that the persons of the Trinity are co-equal and co-eternal, sharing the same divine essence but distinguished by their relations of origin. Augustine described the Trinity as "lover, beloved, and love itself,"[140] pointing to a divine life of communion and perfect relationality. Michael F. Bird affirms that "to experience the salvific blessings of the gospel is to be immersed in a Trinitarian reality," emphasizing that the doctrine is not abstract but lived out in the believer's daily experience.[141]

This theological precision is not mere abstraction; it protects the heart of the gospel. Only if the Son is truly God can He fully reveal the Father and accomplish redemption; only if the Spirit is truly God can He apply salvation to believers and unite them to Christ. The Trinity is thus the framework for

---

[138] William Burt Pope, *A Compendium of Christian Theology*, vol. 1 (London: Beveridge and Co., 1879), 234
[139] Augustus Hopkins Strong, *Systematic Theology* (Philadelphia: American Baptist Publication Society, 1907), 145
[140] Augustine, *The City of God*, trans. Henry Bettenson (London: Penguin Classics, 2003), XIX.17
[141] Michael F. Bird, *Evangelical Theology: A Biblical and Systematic Introduction* (Grand Rapids: Zondervan, 2013), 119

understanding creation, redemption, sanctification, and the ultimate destiny of humanity. To confess God as triune is to confess that love and relationship stand at the center of reality and that human life finds its purpose and fulfillment in communion with this triune God.

Relational Love Within the Godhead

At the heart of the Trinity is a mystery of perfect, eternal love. The Father, Son, and Holy Spirit exist in an unbroken communion of giving and receiving, marked not by competition or hierarchy but by mutual glorification, delight, and love. As theologian Cornelius Plantinga Jr. describes, the Trinity is "a zestful, wondrous community of divine light, love, joy, mutuality, and verve" where each Person centers not on Self but on the Others.[142] This relational love is not peripheral to God's nature — it is God's nature. As 1 John 4:8 declares, "God is love," and within the Trinity, we see love perfectly enacted from eternity past.

This divine communion is beautifully displayed in Jesus' high priestly prayer in John 17, where He speaks of the glory He shares with the Father and prays that His followers would be brought into that same unity: "That they may all be one; just as you, Father, are in me, and I in you" (John 17:21). Here, Jesus does not merely express a wish for human agreement but points to the divine relational pattern that undergirds all Christian community. The Father eternally loves the Son; the Son delights in the Father; and the Spirit is the personal bond of love between them, proceeding from the Father and the Son (John 15:26). This

---

[142] Cornelius Plantinga Jr., *Engaging God's World* (Grand Rapids, MI: Eerdmans, 2002), 30

eternal dynamic sets the pattern for creation and redemption, where love is never mere sentiment but the very essence of divine action.

The Cappadocian Fathers (Basil the Great, Gregory of Nyssa, Gregory of Nazianzus) developed the concept of *perichoresis* — a term describing the mutual indwelling of the three divine persons. This is not a blending of persons but an interpenetration, where each Person fully dwells in the Others without losing individuality. As Gregory of Nazianzus said, "They are each in each other by the power of love and share the same motion."[143] This vision guards against hierarchy and separation, showing that divine unity is not monotony but a dynamic communion of love.

The relational love within the Trinity carries profound implications for human relationships. Made in the image of this God, humanity is designed for communion with God and each other. This is why the New Testament repeatedly grounds ethical commands in Trinitarian patterns: just as the Son submits to the Father (Phil. 2:5–11), so believers are called to mutual submission (Eph. 5:21); just as the Father glorifies the Son, so we are called to honor one another (Rom. 12:10). The doctrine of *perichoresis* thus becomes not just a metaphysical truth but a pastoral guide for Christian life, calling believers into mutual love, service, and deference.

Historically, theologians such as Jonathan Edwards reflected on the beauty of divine love, writing, "God is God because He is a sweet and holy society in Himself." This insight

---

[143] Gregory of Nazianzus, *Orations*, trans. Frederick Williams and Lionel Wickham (Crestwood, NY: St. Vladimir's Seminary Press, 2002), 40

points to the Trinity as the source of all the universe's beauty, goodness, and joy. Contemporary theologians like Miroslav Volf have extended this reflection, suggesting that the Trinity models the kind of inclusive, self-giving community that human societies should aspire to, especially within the church. Rather than mere uniformity or isolated individuality, Christian community is called to mirror the diversity-in-unity of the Triune God, bearing witness to the world of a love that reconciles and restores.

Practically, reflecting Trinitarian love challenges believers to embrace humility, vulnerability, and interdependence. It resists the pull toward isolation, self-promotion, or domination, calling instead for a life patterned after the self-emptying love of Christ. In marriage, friendship, church leadership, and cross-cultural engagement, the doctrine of the Trinity invites us to live with open hearts, seeking the good of the other, and finding joy in mutual glorification rather than self-centered achievement. This relational love has inspired rich theological reflection and spiritual application throughout history. It has been explored in the mystical writings of the Eastern Orthodox tradition, where divine love is seen not only as a doctrine but as a pathway to theosis—participation in the divine life.

Through thinkers like Thomas Aquinas, Western tradition emphasizes unity and distinction in God as the basis for human rationality and moral order. Contemporary theologians draw on Trinitarian love to address social justice, reconciliation, and environmental stewardship, arguing that the relational God calls humans to heal broken relationships in every sphere of life. This expanded vision shows that Trinitarian love is not confined to theology textbooks but pulses through the church's life and the witness of believers worldwide, inspiring humility, courage, and radical love across generations.

Trinitarian Patterns in Christian Life and Community

The reality of the Trinity does not remain locked in theological abstraction; it shapes how Christians live, relate, and worship. To understand the Trinity is to grasp the pattern by which believers are called to live in relation to God and one another. The church, as the community of God's people, reflects the life of the Triune God by embodying unity in diversity, mutual love, and shared purpose. As Paul writes in Ephesians 4:4–6, "There is one body and one Spirit... one Lord, one faith, one baptism, one God and Father of all."[144] This passage beautifully captures the Trinitarian pattern at work within the Christian community: the Spirit binds believers into one body, the Son is the Lord of their confession, and the Father is the source of all life and blessing.

This pattern has profound ethical, spiritual, and relational implications. The Trinity teaches believers to embrace difference without division, to value the unique gifts of others, and to cultivate relationships marked by humility and self-giving love. As Augustine observed, the mutual love within the Godhead is the supreme example for human love: just as the Father, Son, and Spirit glorify and honor one another, so Christians are called to seek the flourishing of one another in families, friendships, and churches.[145] Jonathan Edwards described this love as "a holy

---

[144] Augustine, *On the Trinity*, trans. Edmund Hill (Brooklyn, NY: New City Press, 1991), 214

[145] Jonathan Edwards, *Charity and Its Fruits* (Carlisle, PA: Banner of Truth, 1969), 32

energy" that should animate every aspect of Christian life, from worship to service to mission.[146]

In worship, the Trinitarian pattern invites believers into a rhythm of praise directed to the Father, through the Son, by the power of the Holy Spirit. This dynamic undergirds liturgical traditions, shapes prayer life, and grounds the sacraments. In baptism, believers are immersed into the name of the triune God (Matt. 28:19), signifying their entrance into this divine communion. In the Eucharist, they participate in the life of Christ by the Spirit, offering thanksgiving to the Father.[147]

In mission, the Trinity provides the foundation for how the church engages the world. The Father sends the Son; the Son sends the Spirit; the Spirit empowers the church to bear witness to the gospel. This sending love becomes the template for Christian outreach, characterized not by domination but by invitation, not by coercion but by sacrificial service. As Miroslav Volf argues, the relational nature of the Trinity calls the church to be a community of embrace, extending reconciliation to a fractured world.[148]

Practically, Trinitarian life calls believers to reflect God's relational nature in their daily interactions. This includes cultivating patience, forgiveness, and empathy; building communities marked by hospitality and inclusion; and pursuing justice as an outworking of God's peace. Whether in leadership, discipleship, or everyday friendship, the Trinity offers a vision of

---

[146] Michael F. Bird, *Evangelical Theology* (Grand Rapids, MI: Zondervan, 2013), 137

[147] Miroslav Volf, *After Our Likeness: The Church as the Image of the Trinity* (Grand Rapids, MI: Eerdmans, 1998), 194

[148] Paul, Ephesians 4:4–6

shared life that resists individualism and consumerism, instead calling people into the rich communion of God's love.

Ultimately, the Trinity is not just an object of contemplation but the living source of Christian transformation. As believers are conformed to the image of Christ by the Spirit, they are drawn deeper into the relational life of God, becoming participants in the divine dance of love that will find its consummation in the new creation.

Implications for Worship, Mission, and Everyday Relationships

The doctrine of the Trinity profoundly shapes Christian worship, mission, and relationships, touching every corner of Christian existence. In worship, the triune God is both the subject and the object of praise. Christians address the Father through the Son by the power of the Spirit, entering into the eternal communion of divine love. As James B. Torrance emphasizes, Christian worship is participation in the Son's communion with the Father, enabled by the Spirit, drawing believers into God's life, not merely observing it from afar.[149] This theological dynamic distinguishes Christian worship from mere religious ritual, inviting believers to share in God's own relational life and transforming prayer, song, sacrament, and silence into encounters with divine communion.

In mission, the Trinitarian sending shapes the church's engagement with the world. As the Father sent the Son and the Son sent the Spirit, the church is sent to embody God's love, truth, and reconciliation among the nations. Lesslie Newbigin

---

[149] James B. Torrance, *Worship, Community and the Triune God of Grace* (Downers Grove, IL: InterVarsity Press, 1996), 20

writes, "The mission of the church is the overflow of the love of God in the Trinity into the life of the world."[150] Christian mission, therefore, is not about expanding an institution but extending the embrace of God's relational, restorative love to a broken creation. This perspective deepens the church's understanding of justice, peace, and mercy, viewing these not as isolated social concerns but as the very outworking of the divine nature. The Trinity becomes the lens through which the church discerns its role in global poverty, environmental care, racial reconciliation, and peacemaking across nations.

In everyday relationships, the Trinity offers both a model and a source of transformation. The perichoretic life of the Trinity—that eternal mutual indwelling of Father, Son, and Spirit—becomes a pattern for human communities marked by mutual respect, self-giving, and joyful interdependence. As Catherine Mowry LaCugna observes, "The life of God—precisely because it is triune—does not belong to God alone... but is our destiny as well."[151] In marriage, friendship, family, workplace, and civic life, believers are called to reflect the dynamic of love, humility, and unity they see in the triune God. This includes practices of forgiveness when trust is broken, empathy in the face of suffering, and celebration of diversity as an expression of God's internal communion.

Such a vision resists the individualism and consumerism of modern culture, inviting believers into a countercultural posture of shared life and mutual accountability. It calls believers

---

[150] Lesslie Newbigin, *The Open Secret: An Introduction to the Theology of Mission* (Grand Rapids, MI: Eerdmans, 1995), 27
[151] Catherine Mowry LaCugna, *God for Us: The Trinity and Christian Life* (San Francisco: HarperOne, 1991), 378

into hospitality, forgiveness, service, and reconciliation practices, seeing these as not optional virtues but essential marks of Trinitarian participation. It urges churches to become communities where diversity is embraced, power is exercised in service, and relationships are grounded in grace and truth. The Trinity shapes the church not as a hierarchy of control but as a community of mutual flourishing, where leadership is servant-hearted and discipleship is relational.

Furthermore, the Trinity's implications extend beyond personal piety into life's social, political, and ecological dimensions. It offers a vision of holistic transformation anchored in the relational nature of God, challenging Christians to think about economics, governance, education, and environmental stewardship through a Trinitarian lens. As scholars like Jurgen Moltmann have argued, the doctrine of the Trinity has far-reaching consequences for how Christians resist oppression, promote equality, and envision communities of justice and peace.

Ultimately, to live with a Trinitarian vision is to recognize that all of life is woven into the life of God. Worship flows into mission; mission flows into daily relationships; and daily relationships become the crucible where God's love is made visible. This is not an abstract or theoretical claim but a living truth that continues to inspire believers to walk humbly with God and one another, bearing witness to the relational God who makes all things new.

Conclusion: Living Bold Faith in the Light of the Trinity

Living with a Kingdom vision anchored in the Trinity is not merely about intellectual affirmation but a transformed existence marked by bold, embodied faith. To confess the triune

God is to declare that love, communion, and mission stand at the center of reality, and that believers are called to mirror these divine realities in their daily walk. Bold faith is not reckless triumphalism but courageous participation in God's redemptive story, grounded in the eternal communion of Father, Son, and Spirit.

At its heart, bold faith means trusting in the Father's sovereign goodness even when circumstances are uncertain. It means following the Son in radical discipleship, embracing the cross and the costly path of love. It means depending on the Spirit for wisdom, power, and perseverance, knowing that human strength alone cannot sustain the Christian journey. As Jurgen Moltmann reflects, "The Christian hope embraces the resurrection of the dead and the life of the world to come... it is an active hope, transforming the present in the light of the future promised by God."[152] Bold faith draws its courage from this eschatological horizon, living today in the assurance of God's final victory.

Such faith transforms personal spirituality, community life, and public witness. I believe it cultivates practices of prayer, Scripture engagement, and sacramental participation that immerse believers in the triune life. Community fosters unity, mutual accountability, and creative collaboration, reflecting the relationality of God. Publicly, it inspires acts of justice, mercy, and peacemaking, bearing witness to a God whose love overflows beyond the boundaries of the church.

---

[152] Jurgen Moltmann, *Theology of Hope* (Minneapolis, MN: Fortress Press, 1993), 42

Bold faith also means embracing vulnerability and humility. It acknowledges human limits and leans into God's sufficiency, confessing with Paul, "When I am weak, then I am strong" (2 Cor. 12:10). It means daring to love enemies, forgive offenders, speak truth to power, and risk reputation or comfort for the sake of Christ's mission. It also means persevering through doubt, suffering, and loss, trusting that the triune God holds all things in love and is weaving even pain into His redemptive purposes.

In the end, living with bold faith in light of the Trinity is to echo the prayer of Jesus in John 17: that believers may be one as He and the Father are one, that they may share in His glory, and that the love with which the Father has loved the Son may be in them. This is the radiant horizon of the Christian life — not individual achievement but union with the triune God, participation in His life, and joyful embodiment of His love in the world.

Conclusion

Dwelling with God Forever

From the opening garden of Eden to the radiant city of the New Jerusalem, the story of Scripture has revealed one central theme: God's unrelenting desire to dwell with His people. Though sin fractured communion in the garden, the Lord's presence has continually broken into history—through covenant, temple, incarnation, Spirit, and Church—pointing toward the day when His dwelling will be complete.

As we have traced this journey, we are reminded that God's presence is not merely a theological concept but a lived reality. To abide with Him is to live in daily communion, embody holiness, persevere in faith, and participate in His Kingdom mission. Every stage of redemptive history calls us to live as a people marked by His presence, bearing witness to the world that the dwelling place of God is with humanity.

The final vision in Revelation 21–22 assures us that what was lost in Eden will be restored beyond measure: God Himself will be with us, His people, and we will see His face. This is the hope that sustains us, the promise that empowers us, and the destiny toward which all creation groans. Until that day, our task is straightforward: to live now as God's dwelling place—temples of His Spirit, communities of His Kingdom, and ambassadors of His presence in a world longing for redemption.

May this book not simply inform your mind but awaken your heart to live faithfully in God's presence, anticipating the glory to come and embodying His nearness in the present. The Kingdom of God is here, and the dwelling place of God is being revealed—in us, through us, and one day, in fullness forever.

NOTES

Chapter 1

[1] Hamilton, Victor P. 1990. The Book of Genesis, Chapters 1–17. Grand Rapids: Eerdmans. Pg. 140

[2] Augustine. [398] 1998. *Confessions*. Translated by Henry Chadwick. Oxford: Oxford University Press.

[3] Benedict. [c. 540] 1981. *The Rule of St. Benedict*. Collegeville, MN: Liturgical Press.

[4] Teresa of Ávila. [1577] 1961. *The Interior Castle*. Translated by E. Allison Peers. Garden City, NY: Doubleday.

[5] Calvin, John. [1559] 2008. *Institutes of the Christian Religion*. Translated by Henry Beveridge. Peabody, MA: Hendrickson Publishers.

[6] Lawrence, Brother. [1692] 2005. *The Practice of the Presence of God*. Mineola, NY: Dover Publications

[7] Taylor, Charles. 2007. *A Secular Age*. Cambridge, MA: Harvard University Press.

[8] Willard, Dallas. 1998. *The Spirit of the Disciplines*. San Francisco: HarperOne.

[9] Foster, Richard. 1978. *Celebration of Discipline: The Path to Spiritual Growth*. San Francisco: Harper & Row.

[10] Packer, J.I. 1993. *Knowing God*. Downers Grove, IL: InterVarsity Press.

Athanasius. [c. 318] 1998. *On the Incarnation*. Translated by John Behr. Yonkers, NY: St. Vladimir's Seminary Press.

Chapter 2

[1] Willard, Dallas. 1998. *The Spirit of the Disciplines: Understanding How God Changes Lives*. San Francisco: HarperSanFrancisco

[2] Calvin, John. [1559] 2008. *Institutes of the Christian Religion*. Translated by Henry Beveridge. Peabody, MA: Hendrickson Publishers.

[3] Luther, Martin. 1966. *Luther's Works, Vol. 35: Word and Sacrament I*. Edited by E. Theodore Bachmann. Philadelphia: Fortress Press.

[4] Calvin, John. [1559] 2008. *Institutes of the Christian Religion*. Translated by Henry Beveridge. Peabody, MA: Hendrickson Publishers

[5] Bonhoeffer, Dietrich. 1954. *Life Together*. Translated by John W. Doberstein. New York: Harper & Row.

[6] Taylor, Charles. 2007. *A Secular Age*. Cambridge, MA: Harvard University Press.

[7] Origen. 1973. *Origen: An Exhortation to Martyrdom, Prayer, and Selected Works*. Translated by Rowan A. Greer. New York: Paulist Press.

[8] Taylor, Charles. 2007. *A Secular Age*. Cambridge, MA: Harvard University Press.

[9] Origen. 1973. *Origen: An Exhortation to Martyrdom, Prayer, and Selected Works*. Translated by Rowan A. Greer. New York:

Paulist Press.

[10] Luther, Martin. 1966. *Luther's Works, Vol. 35: Word and Sacrament I*. Edited by E. Theodore Bachmann. Philadelphia: Fortress Press

[11] Calvin, John. [1559] 2008. *Institutes of the Christian Religion*. Translated by Henry Beveridge. Peabody, MA: Hendrickson Publishers.

[12] Bonhoeffer, Dietrich. 1954. *Life Together*. Translated by John W. Doberstein. New York: Harper & Row.

[13] Willard, Dallas. 1998. *The Spirit of the Disciplines: Understanding How God Changes Lives*. San Francisco: HarperSanFrancisco

[14] Willard, Dallas. 1998. *The Spirit of the Disciplines: Understanding How God Changes Lives*. San Francisco: HarperSanFrancisco

[15] Taylor, Charles. 2007. *A Secular Age*. Cambridge, MA: Harvard University Press.

[16] Bonhoeffer, Dietrich. 1954. *Life Together*. Translated by John W. Doberstein. New York: Harper & Row.

Chapter 3

[1] Bonhoeffer, Dietrich. 1954. *Life Together*. Translated by John W. Doberstein. New York: Harper & Row.

[2] Willard, Dallas. 1998. *The Spirit of the Disciplines: Understanding How God Changes Lives*. San Francisco: Harper, San Francisco.

[3] Calvin, John. [1559] 2008. *Institutes of the Christian Religion*. Translated by Henry Beveridge. Peabody, MA: Hendrickson Publishers.

[4] Augustine. [397] 1998. *Confessions*. Translated by Henry Chadwick. Oxford: Oxford University Press.

[5] Luther, Martin. 1966. *Luther's Works, Vol. 35: Word and Sacrament I*. Edited by E. Theodore Bachmann. Philadelphia: Fortress Press.

[6] Calvin, John. [1559] 2008. *Institutes of the Christian Religion*. Translated by Henry Beveridge. Peabody, MA: Hendrickson Publishers.

[7] Bonhoeffer, Dietrich. 1954. *Life Together*. Translated by John W. Doberstein. New York: Harper & Row.

[8] Willard, Dallas. 1998. *The Spirit of the Disciplines: Understanding How God Changes Lives*. San Francisco: Harper, San Francisco.

Chapter 4

[1] Calvin, John. [1559] 2008. *Institutes of the Christian Religion*. Translated by Henry Beveridge. Peabody, MA: Hendrickson Publishers.

[2] Augustine. [397] 1998. *Confessions*. Translated by Henry Chadwick. Oxford: Oxford University Press.

[3] Luther, Martin. 1966. *Luther's Works, Vol. 35: Word and Sacrament I*. Edited by E. Theodore Bachmann. Philadelphia: Fortress Press.

[4] Calvin, John. [1559] 2008. *Institutes of the Christian Religion.* Translated by Henry Beveridge. Peabody, MA: Hendrickson Publishers.

[5] Bonhoeffer, Dietrich. 1954. *Life Together.* Translated by John W. Doberstein. New York: Harper & Row.

6 Willard, Dallas. 1998. *The Spirit of the Disciplines: Understanding How God Changes Lives.* San Francisco: HarperSanFrancisco.

Chapter 5

[1] Calvin, John. [1559] 2008. *Institutes of the Christian Religion.* Translated by Henry Beveridge. Peabody, MA: Hendrickson Publishers.

[2] Augustine. [397] 1998. *Confessions.* Translated by Henry Chadwick. Oxford: Oxford University Press.

[3] Bonhoeffer, Dietrich. 1954. *Life Together.* Translated by John W. Doberstein. New York: Harper & Row.

[4] Willard, Dallas. 1998. *The Spirit of the Disciplines: Understanding How God Changes Lives.* San Francisco: HarperSanFrancisco.

[5] Augustine. [397] 1998. *Confessions.* Translated by Henry Chadwick. Oxford: Oxford University Press.

[6] Luther, Martin. 1966. *Luther's Works, Vol. 35: Word and Sacrament I.* Edited by E. Theodore Bachmann. Philadelphia: Fortress Press.

[7] Calvin, John. [1559] 2008. *Institutes of the Christian Religion.* Translated by Henry Beveridge. Peabody, MA: Hendrickson Publishers.

[8] Willard, Dallas. 1998. *The Spirit of the Disciplines: Understanding How God Changes Lives.* San Francisco: HarperSanFrancisco.

Chapter 6

[1] John Owen, *Overcoming Sin and Temptation*, ed. Kelly M. Kapic and Justin Taylor (Wheaton, IL: Crossway, 2006), 50

[2] Athanasius of Alexandria, *On the Incarnation*, ed. and trans. A Religious of C.S.M.V. (Crestwood, NY: St. Vladimir's Seminary Press, 1993), 54

[3] Gregory of Nyssa, "The Life of Moses," in *From Glory to Glory: Texts from Gregory of Nyssa's Mystical Writings*, selected by Jean Daniélou, trans. Herbert Musurillo (New York: Charles Scribner's Sons, 1961), 105–9.

[4] Thomas à Kempis, *The Imitation of Christ*, trans. Aloysius Croft and Harold Bolton (Mineola, NY: Dover Publications, 2003), Book 1, ch. 1.

[5] John Wesley, *A Plain Account of Christian Perfection* (Kansas City, MO: Beacon Hill Press, 1966), 51

[6] Kevin DeYoung, "The Pastor's Personal Holiness," *The Gospel Coalition* (blog), July 23, 2015

[7] Richard J. Foster, *Celebration of Discipline: The Path to Spiritual Growth* (San Francisco: Harper & Row, 1978), 2.

[8] Ibid., 33

[9] Henri J. M. Nouwen, *The Way of the Heart: Desert Spirituality and Contemporary Ministry* (New York: Seabury Press, 1981), 15

[10] Foster, *Celebration of Discipline*, 2

[11] C. S. Lewis, *Mere Christianity* (New York: HarperCollins, 2001), 122

[12] Ibid., 123

[13] 1 Kevin DeYoung, "The Pastor's Personal Holiness," *The Gospel Coalition* (blog), July 23, 2015

Chapter 7

[1] J.I. Packer, Knowing God (Downers Grove, IL: InterVarsity Press, 1973), 231.

[2] Robert Alter, The Art of Biblical Narrative (New York: Basic Books, 1981).

[3] John Goldingay, Old Testament Theology: Israel's Gospel (Downers Grove, IL: IVP Academic, 2003).

[4] Timothy Keller, Walking with God through Pain and Suffering (New York: Penguin Books, 2015).

[5] Gordon D. Fee, Paul, the Spirit, and the People of God (Peabody, MA: Hendrickson, 1996).

[6] N. T. Wright, The Day the Revolution Began: Reconsidering the Meaning of Jesus's Crucifixion (San Francisco: HarperOne, 2016).

[7] Dietrich Bonhoeffer, Letters and Papers from Prison (New York: Touchstone, 1997).

[8] J.B. Lightfoot and J.R. Harmer, The Apostolic Fathers (Grand Rapids, MI: Baker Book House, 1989).

[9] St. Benedict, The Rule of St. Benedict, trans. Timothy Fry (Collegeville, MN: Liturgical Press, 1981).

[10] Martin Luther, The Freedom of a Christian, trans. Mark Tranvik (Minneapolis, MN: Fortress Press, 2008).

[11] John Calvin, Institutes of the Christian Religion, ed. John T. McNeill, trans. Ford Lewis Battles (Philadelphia: Westminster Press, 1960).

[12] Dietrich Bonhoeffer, Ethics, trans. Clifford J. Green (Minneapolis, MN: Fortress Press, 2005).

[13] Corrie ten Boom, The Hiding Place (Grand Rapids, MI: Chosen Books, 1971).

Chapter 8

[1] G. K. Beale, The Temple and the Church's Mission (Downers Grove, IL: IVP Academic, 2004).

[2] N. T. Wright, Matthew for Everyone, Part 2 (Louisville, KY: Westminster John Knox, 2004).

[3] Craig S. Keener, Acts: An Exegetical Commentary, vol. 1 (Grand Rapids, MI: Baker Academic, 2012).

[4] Sandra L. Richter, The Epic of Eden (Downers Grove, IL: IVP Academic, 2008).

[5] George Eldon Ladd, A Theology of the New Testament (Grand Rapids, MI: Eerdmans, 1993).

[6] Herman Ridderbos, Paul: An Outline of His Theology (Grand Rapids, MI: Eerdmans, 1975).

[7] Michael S. Heiser, The Unseen Realm (Bellingham, WA: Lexham Press, 2015).

[8] Thomas R. Schreiner, Paul: Apostle of God's Glory in Christ (Downers Grove, IL: IVP Academic, 2001).

[9] Dallas Willard, The Spirit of the Disciplines (San Francisco: Harper & Row, 1988).

[10] Ignatius of Antioch, The Epistles of Ignatius, in Early Christian Writings, trans. Andrew Louth (London: Penguin, 1987), 107–110.

[11] Bede, Ecclesiastical History of the English People, trans. Leo Sherley Price (London: Penguin Classics, 1990), 172–176.

[12] Martin Luther, The Freedom of a Christian, trans. Mark Tranvik (Minneapolis, MN: Fortress Press, 2008), 50–52.

[13] John Calvin, Institutes of the Christian Religion, ed. John T. McNeill, trans. Ford Lewis Battles (Philadelphia: Westminster Press, 1960), 1.7.4.

[14] John Wesley, The Works of John Wesley (Grand Rapids, MI: Baker, 1986), 13:258.

[15] Allan Anderson, An Introduction to Pentecostalism: Global Charismatic Christianity (Cambridge: Cambridge University Press, 2013), 45–60.

Chapter 9

[1] Reeves, Michael. *Delighting in the Trinity*. Downers Grove, IL: InterVarsity Press, 2012.

[2] Bonhoeffer, Dietrich. *Life Together*. Translated by John W. Doberstein. New York: Harper & Row, 1954.

Chapter 10

[1] Wright, N.T. *How God Became King: The Forgotten Story of the Gospels*. New York: HarperOne, 2012.

[2] Volf, Miroslav. *Exclusion and Embrace: A Theological Exploration of Identity, Otherness, and Reconciliation*. Nashville: Abingdon Press, 1996.

[3] Foster, Richard. *Freedom of Simplicity*. San Francisco: Harper & Row, 1981.

[4] Willard, Dallas. *The Spirit of the Disciplines: Understanding How God Changes Lives*. San Francisco: Harper & Row, 1988.

[5] Bonhoeffer, Dietrich. *Life Together*. New York: Harper & Row, 1954.

Chapter 11

[1] Randy Alcorn, Managing God's Money: A Biblical Guide (Carol Stream, IL: Tyndale, 2005).

[2] Timothy Keller, Every Good Endeavor: Connecting Your Work to God's Work (New York: Dutton, 2012).

[3] George Barna, The State of the Church 2018 (Ventura, CA: Barna Group, 2018).

[4] Donald S. Whitney, Spiritual Disciplines for the Christian Life (Colorado Springs: NavPress, 2014).

[5] James K. A. Smith, Desiring the Kingdom: Worship, Worldview, and Cultural Formation (Grand Rapids: Baker Academic, 2009).

[6] Peter Scazzero, Emotionally Healthy Discipleship (Grand Rapids: Zondervan, 2021).

Chapter 12

[1] John C. Maxwell, *The 21 Irrefutable Laws of Leadership* (Nashville: Thomas Nelson, 2007), 56.

[2] Henry and Richard Blackaby, *Spiritual Leadership: Moving People to God's Agenda* (Nashville: B&H Publishing, 2011), 73.

[3] Dallas Willard, *The Divine Conspiracy: Rediscovering Our Hidden Life in God* (San Francisco: HarperOne, 2009), 258.

[4] J. Oswald Sanders, *Spiritual Leadership: Principles of Excellence for Every Believer* (Chicago: Moody Publishers, 2007), 112.

[5] A.W. Tozer, *The Pursuit of God* (Harrisburg: Christian Publications, 1982), 84.

Chapter 13

[1] Joseph Pieper, *The Four Cardinal Virtues* (Notre Dame, IN: University of Notre Dame Press, 1966), 128.

[2] John Ortberg, *If You Want to Walk on Water, You Have Got to Get Out of the Boat* (Grand Rapids: Zondervan, 2001), 57.

[3] N.T. Wright, *After You Believe: Why Christian Character Matters* (New York: HarperOne, 2010), 134.

[4] Dallas Willard, *The Spirit of the Disciplines: Understanding How God Changes Lives* (San Francisco: HarperOne, 1999), 202.

Chapter 14

[1] Christopher J. H. Wright, *The Mission of God: Unlocking the Bible's Grand Narrative* (Downers Grove, IL: IVP Academic, 2006), 62.

[2] Lesslie Newbigin, *The Gospel in a Pluralist Society* (Grand Rapids, MI: Eerdmans, 1989), 227.

[3] John Stott, *The Radical Disciple* (Downers Grove, IL: InterVarsity Press, 2010), 88.

[4] Michael F. Bird, *Evangelical Theology: A Biblical and Systematic Introduction*, 2nd ed. (Grand Rapids, MI: Zondervan Academic, 2020), 509.

[5] Christopher J. H. Wright, *The Mission of God's People: A Biblical Theology of the Church's Mission* (Grand Rapids, MI: Zondervan, 2010), 25.

[6] Eckhard J. Schnabel, *Paul the Missionary: Realities, Strategies, and Methods* (Downers Grove, IL: IVP Academic, 2008), 306.

[7] D. A. Carson, *The Gospel According to John* (Leicester, England: Inter-Varsity Press; Grand Rapids, MI: Eerdmans, 1991), 225.

[8] Craig S. Keener, *Acts: An Exegetical Commentary*, vol. 2 (Grand Rapids, MI: Baker Academic, 2013), 1544.

[9] Timothy Keller, *Center Church: Doing Balanced, Gospel-Centered Ministry in Your City* (Grand Rapids, MI: Zondervan, 2012), 221.

[10] David F. Wells, *God in the Whirlwind: How the Holy-love of God Reorients Our World* (Wheaton, IL: Crossway, 2014), 56.

[11] William Lane Craig, *On Guard: Defending Your Faith with Reason and Precision* (Colorado Springs, CO: David C. Cook, 2010), 35.

[12] Os Guinness, *Fool's Talk: Recovering the Art of Christian Persuasion* (Downers Grove, IL: IVP Books, 2015), 112.

[13] John Stott, *The Message of Ephesians* (Downers Grove, IL: InterVarsity Press, 1979), 260.

[14] Michael Frost, *Surprise the World: The Five Habits of Highly Missional People* (Colorado Springs, CO: NavPress, 2016), 57.

[15] Andrew F. Walls, *The Missionary Movement in Christian History: Studies in the Transmission of Faith* (Maryknoll, NY: Orbis Books, 1996), 15.

[16] J. I. Packer, *Evangelism and the Sovereignty of God* (Downers Grove, IL: IVP, 1961), 27.

[17] Greg Koukl, *Tactics: A Game Plan for Discussing Your Christian Convictions* (Grand Rapids, MI: Zondervan, 2009), 41.

[18] Rebecca Manley Pippert, *Out of the Saltshaker and into the World: Evangelism as a Way of Life* (Downers Grove, IL: IVP, 1999), 23.

[19] Christopher J. H. Wright, *The Mission of God's People: A Biblical Theology of the Church's Mission* (Grand Rapids, MI: Zondervan, 2010), 215.

[20] Michael Green, *Evangelism in the Early Church* (Grand Rapids, MI: Eerdmans, 2004), 12

Chapter 15

[1] John Calvin, *Institutes of the Christian Religion*, trans. Henry Beveridge (Peabody, MA: Hendrickson, 2008), III.25.

[2] N. T. Wright, *After You Believe: Why Christian Character Matters* (New York: HarperOne, 2010), 115.

[3] Jürgen Moltmann, *Theology of Hope* (Minneapolis, MN: Fortress Press, 1993), 23.

[4] Miroslav Volf, *A Public Faith: How Followers of Christ Should Serve the Common Good* (Grand Rapids, MI: Brazos Press, 2011), 65.

[5] Rowan Williams, *Being Christian* (Grand Rapids, MI: Eerdmans, 2014), 45.

[6] N. T. Wright, *After You Believe: Why Christian Character Matters* (New York: HarperOne, 2010), 115.

[7] Dietrich Bonhoeffer, *The Cost of Discipleship* (New York: Macmillan, 1959), 44.

[8] Jürgen Moltmann, *Theology of Hope* (Minneapolis, MN: Fortress Press, 1993), 35.

[9] Corrie ten Boom, *The Hiding Place* (Grand Rapids, MI: Chosen Books, 1971), 217.

[10] Lesslie Newbigin, *The Gospel in a Pluralist Society* (Grand Rapids, MI: Eerdmans, 1989), 110.

[11] Augustine, *The City of God*, trans. Henry Bettenson (London: Penguin Classics, 2003), XIX.17.

[12] James Davison Hunter, *To Change the World: The Irony, Tragedy, and Possibility of Christianity in the Late Modern World* (New York: Oxford University Press, 2010), 243.

[13] Timothy Keller, *Center Church: Doing Balanced, Gospel-Centered Ministry in Your City* (Grand Rapids, MI: Zondervan, 2012), 290.

Chapter 16

[1] William Burt Pope, *A Compendium of Christian Theology*, vol. 1 (London: Beveridge and Co., 1879), 234.

[2] Augustus Hopkins Strong, *Systematic Theology* (Philadelphia: American Baptist Publication Society, 1907), 145.

[3] Augustine, *The City of God*, trans. Henry Bettenson (London: Penguin Classics, 2003), XIX.17. [4] Michael F. Bird, *Evangelical Theology: A Biblical and Systematic Introduction* (Grand Rapids: Zondervan, 2013), 119.

[5] Cornelius Plantinga Jr., *Engaging God's World* (Grand Rapids, MI: Eerdmans, 2002), 30.

[6] Gregory of Nazianzus, *Orations*, trans. Frederick Williams and Lionel Wickham (Crestwood, NY: St. Vladimir's Seminary Press, 2002), 40.

[7] Augustine, *On the Trinity*, trans. Edmund Hill (Brooklyn, NY: New City Press, 1991), 214.
[8] Jonathan Edwards, *Charity and Its Fruits* (Carlisle, PA: Banner of Truth, 1969), 32.
[9] Michael F. Bird, *Evangelical Theology* (Grand Rapids, MI: Zondervan, 2013), 137.
[10] Miroslav Volf, *After Our Likeness: The Church as the Image of the Trinity* (Grand Rapids, MI: Eerdmans, 1998), 194.
[11] Paul, Ephesians 4:4–6.

[12] James B. Torrance, *Worship, Community and the Triune God of Grace* (Downers Grove, IL: InterVarsity Press, 1996), 20.
[13] Lesslie Newbigin, *The Open Secret: An Introduction to the Theology of Mission* (Grand Rapids, MI: Eerdmans, 1995), 27.
[14] Catherine Mowry LaCugna, *God for Us: The Trinity and Christian Life* (San Francisco: HarperOne, 1991), 378.

[15] Jurgen Moltmann, *Theology of Hope* (Minneapolis, MN: Fortress Press, 1993), 42.

Bibliography

Alcorn, Randy. *Managing God's Money: A Biblical Guide*. Carol Stream, IL: Tyndale, 2005.

Alter, Robert. *The Art of Biblical Narrative*. New York: Basic Books, 1981.

Anderson, Allan. *An Introduction to Pentecostalism: Global Charismatic Christianity*. Cambridge: Cambridge University Press, 2013.

Athanasius. *On the Incarnation*. Translated by John Behr. Yonkers, NY: St. Vladimir's Seminary Press, [c. 318] 1998.

Athanasius of Alexandria. *On the Incarnation*. Edited and translated by a Religious of C.S.M.V. Crestwood, NY: St. Vladimir's Seminary Press, 1993.

Augustine. *Confessions*. Translated by Henry Chadwick. Oxford: Oxford University Press, [398] 1998.

———. *On the Trinity*. Translated by Edmund Hill. Brooklyn, NY: New City Press, 1991.

———. *The City of God*. Translated by Henry Bettenson. London: Penguin Classics, 2003.

Barna, George. *The State of the Church 2018*. Ventura, CA: Barna Group, 2018.

Beale, G. K. *The Temple and the Church's Mission*. Downers Grove, IL: IVP Academic, 2004.

Bede. *Ecclesiastical History of the English People*. Translated by Leo Sherley-Price. London: Penguin Classics, 1990.

Benedict. *The Rule of St. Benedict*. Collegeville, MN: Liturgical Press, [c. 540] 1981.

Bird, Michael F. *Evangelical Theology: A Biblical and Systematic Introduction*. Grand Rapids, MI: Zondervan, 2013.

———. *Evangelical Theology: A Biblical and Systematic Introduction*. 2nd ed. Grand Rapids, MI: Zondervan Academic, 2020.

Blackaby, Henry, and Richard Blackaby. *Spiritual Leadership: Moving People to God's Agenda*. Nashville: B&H Publishing, 2011.

Bonhoeffer, Dietrich. *Ethics*. Translated by Clifford J. Green. Minneapolis, MN: Fortress Press, 2005.

———. *Letters and Papers from Prison*. New York: Touchstone, 1997.

———. *Life Together*. Translated by John W. Doberstein. New York: Harper & Row, 1954.

———. *The Cost of Discipleship*. New York: Macmillan, 1959.

Calvin, John. *Institutes of the Christian Religion*. Edited by John T. McNeill. Translated by Ford Lewis Battles. Philadelphia: Westminster Press, 1960.

————. *Institutes of the Christian Religion*. Translated by Henry Beveridge. Peabody, MA: Hendrickson Publishers, [1559] 2008.

Carson, D. A. *The Gospel According to John*. Leicester, England: Inter-Varsity Press; Grand Rapids, MI: Eerdmans, 1991.

Craig, William Lane. *On Guard: Defending Your Faith with Reason and Precision*. Colorado Springs, CO: David C. Cook, 2010.

DeYoung, Kevin. "The Pastor's Personal Holiness." *The Gospel Coalition* (blog), July 23, 2015.

Edwards, Jonathan. *Charity and Its Fruits*. Carlisle, PA: Banner of Truth, 1969.

Fee, Gordon D. *Paul, the Spirit, and the People of God*. Peabody, MA: Hendrickson, 1996.

Foster, Richard J. *Celebration of Discipline: The Path to Spiritual Growth*. San Francisco: Harper & Row, 1978.

————. *Freedom of Simplicity*. San Francisco: Harper & Row, 1981.

Frost, Michael. *Surprise the World: The Five Habits of Highly Missional People*. Colorado Springs, CO: NavPress, 2016.

Goldingay, John. *Old Testament Theology: Israel's Gospel*. Downers Grove, IL: IVP Academic, 2003.

Green, Michael. *Evangelism in the Early Church*. Grand Rapids, MI: Eerdmans, 2004.

Gregory of Nazianzus. *Orations*. Translated by Frederick Williams and Lionel Wickham. Crestwood, NY: St. Vladimir's Seminary Press, 2002.

Gregory of Nyssa. "The Life of Moses." In *From Glory to Glory: Texts from Gregory of Nyssa's Mystical Writings*, selected by Jean Daniélou, translated by Herbert Musurillo. New York: Charles Scribner's Sons, 1961.

Guinness, Os. *Fool's Talk: Recovering the Art of Christian Persuasion*. Downers Grove, IL: IVP Books, 2015.

Hamilton, Victor P. *The Book of Genesis, Chapters 1–17*. Grand Rapids: Eerdmans, 1990.

Heiser, Michael S. *The Unseen Realm*. Bellingham, WA: Lexham Press, 2015.

Hunter, James Davison. *To Change the World: The Irony, Tragedy, and Possibility of Christianity in the Late Modern World*. New York: Oxford University Press, 2010.

Ignatius of Antioch. *The Epistles of Ignatius*. In *Early Christian Writings*, translated by Andrew Louth. London: Penguin, 1987.

Keener, Craig S. *Acts: An Exegetical Commentary*. Vol. 1. Grand Rapids, MI: Baker Academic, 2012.

———. *Acts: An Exegetical Commentary*. Vol. 2. Grand Rapids, MI: Baker Academic, 2013.

Keller, Timothy. *Center Church: Doing Balanced, Gospel-Centered Ministry in Your City*. Grand Rapids, MI: Zondervan, 2012.

———. *Every Good Endeavor: Connecting Your Work to God's Work*. New York: Dutton, 2012.

———. *Walking with God through Pain and Suffering*. New York: Penguin Books, 2015.

Kempis, Thomas à. *The Imitation of Christ*. Translated by Aloysius Croft and Harold Bolton. Mineola, NY: Dover Publications, 2003.

Koukl, Greg. *Tactics: A Game Plan for Discussing Your Christian Convictions*. Grand Rapids, MI: Zondervan, 2009.

LaCugna, Catherine Mowry. *God for Us: The Trinity and Christian Life*. San Francisco: HarperOne, 1991.

Ladd, George Eldon. *A Theology of the New Testament*. Grand Rapids, MI: Eerdmans, 1993.

Lawrence, Brother. *The Practice of the Presence of God*. Mineola, NY: Dover Publications, [1692] 2005.

Lewis, C. S. *Mere Christianity*. New York: HarperCollins, 2001.

Lightfoot, J. B., and J. R. Harmer. *The Apostolic Fathers*. Grand Rapids, MI: Baker Book House, 1989.

Luther, Martin. *Luther's Works*. Vol. 35: *Word and Sacrament I*. Edited by E. Theodore Bachmann. Philadelphia: Fortress Press, 1966.

———. *The Freedom of a Christian*. Translated by Mark Tranvik. Minneapolis, MN: Fortress Press, 2008.

Maxwell, John C. *The 21 Irrefutable Laws of Leadership*. Nashville: Thomas Nelson, 2007.

Moltmann, Jürgen. *Theology of Hope*. Minneapolis, MN: Fortress Press, 1993.

Newbigin, Lesslie. *The Gospel in a Pluralist Society*. Grand Rapids, MI: Eerdmans, 1989.

———. *The Open Secret: An Introduction to the Theology of Mission*. Grand Rapids, MI: Eerdmans, 1995.

Nouwen, Henri J. M. *The Way of the Heart: Desert Spirituality and Contemporary Ministry*. New York: Seabury Press, 1981.

Origen. *Origen: An Exhortation to Martyrdom, Prayer, and Selected Works*. Translated by Rowan A. Greer. New York: Paulist Press, 1973.

Ortberg, John. *If You Want to Walk on Water, You Have Got to Get Out of the Boat*. Grand Rapids: Zondervan, 2001.

Owen, John. *Overcoming Sin and Temptation*. Edited by Kelly M. Kapic and Justin Taylor. Wheaton, IL: Crossway, 2006.

Packer, J. I. *Evangelism and the Sovereignty of God*. Downers Grove, IL: IVP, 1961.

———. *Knowing God*. Downers Grove, IL: InterVarsity Press, 1993.

Pieper, Joseph. *The Four Cardinal Virtues*. Notre Dame, IN: University of Notre Dame Press, 1966.

Pippert, Rebecca Manley. *Out of the Saltshaker and into the World: Evangelism as a Way of Life*. Downers Grove, IL: IVP, 1999.

Plantinga, Cornelius, Jr. *Engaging God's World*. Grand
Rapids, MI: Eerdmans, 2002.

Pope, William Burt. *A Compendium of Christian Theology*.
Vol. 1. London: Beveridge and Co., 1879.

Reeves, Michael. *Delighting in the Trinity*. Downers Grove,
IL: InterVarsity Press, 2012.

Richter, Sandra L. *The Epic of Eden*. Downers Grove, IL:
IVP Academic, 2008.

Ridderbos, Herman. *Paul: An Outline of His Theology*.
Grand Rapids, MI: Eerdmans, 1975.

Sanders, J. Oswald. *Spiritual Leadership: Principles of
Excellence for Every Believer*. Chicago: Moody
Publishers, 2007.

Scazzero, Peter. *Emotionally Healthy Discipleship*. Grand
Rapids: Zondervan, 2021.

Schnabel, Eckhard J. *Paul the Missionary: Realities,
Strategies, and Methods*. Downers Grove, IL: IVP
Academic, 2008.

Schreiner, Thomas R. *Paul: Apostle of God's Glory in Christ*.
Downers Grove, IL: IVP Academic, 2001.

Smith, James K. A. *Desiring the Kingdom: Worship,
Worldview, and Cultural Formation*. Grand Rapids,
MI: Baker Academic, 2009.

Stott, John. *The Message of Ephesians*. Downers Grove, IL:
InterVarsity Press, 1979.

———. *The Radical Disciple*. Downers Grove, IL:
InterVarsity Press, 2010.

Strong, Augustus Hopkins. *Systematic Theology*. Philadelphia: American Baptist Publication Society, 1907.

Taylor, Charles. *A Secular Age*. Cambridge, MA: Harvard University Press, 2007.

Ten Boom, Corrie. *The Hiding Place*. Grand Rapids, MI: Chosen Books, 1971.

Teresa of Ávila. *The Interior Castle*. Translated by E. Allison Peers. Garden City, NY: Doubleday, [1577] 1961.

Thomas à Kempis. *The Imitation of Christ*. Translated by Aloysius Croft and Harold Bolton. Mineola, NY: Dover Publications, 2003.

Torrance, James B. *Worship, Community and the Triune God of Grace*. Downers Grove, IL: InterVarsity Press, 1996.

Tozer, A. W. *The Pursuit of God*. Harrisburg: Christian Publications, 1982.

Volf, Miroslav. *After Our Likeness: The Church as the Image of the Trinity*. Grand Rapids, MI: Eerdmans, 1998.

———. *Exclusion and Embrace: A Theological Exploration of Identity, Otherness, and Reconciliation*. Nashville: Abingdon Press, 1996.

———. *A Public Faith: How Followers of Christ Should Serve the Common Good*. Grand Rapids, MI: Brazos Press, 2011.

Walls, Andrew F. *The Missionary Movement in Christian History: Studies in the Transmission of Faith*. Maryknoll, NY: Orbis Books, 1996.

Wells, David F. *God in the Whirlwind: How the Holy-Love of God Reorients Our World*. Wheaton, IL: Crossway, 2014.

Wesley, John. *A Plain Account of Christian Perfection*. Kansas City, MO: Beacon Hill Press, 1966.

———. *The Works of John Wesley*. Grand Rapids, MI: Baker, 1986.

Whitney, Donald S. *Spiritual Disciplines for the Christian Life*. Colorado Springs: NavPress, 2014.

Willard, Dallas. *The Divine Conspiracy: Rediscovering Our Hidden Life in God*. San Francisco: HarperOne, 2009.

———. *The Spirit of the Disciplines*. San Francisco: Harper & Row, 1988.

———. *The Spirit of the Disciplines: Understanding How God Changes Lives*. San Francisco: HarperSanFrancisco, 1998.

———. *The Spirit of the Disciplines: Understanding How God Changes Lives*. San Francisco: HarperOne, 1999.

Williams, Rowan. *Being Christian*. Grand Rapids, MI: Eerdmans, 2014.

Wright, Christopher J. H. *The Mission of God: Unlocking the Bible's Grand Narrative*. Downers Grove, IL: IVP Academic, 2006.

———. *The Mission of God's People: A Biblical Theology of the Church's Mission*. Grand Rapids, MI: Zondervan, 2010.

Wright, N. T. *After You Believe: Why Christian Character Matters*. New York: HarperOne, 2010.

———. *How God Became King: The Forgotten Story of the Gospels*. New York: HarperOne, 2012.

———. *Matthew for Everyone, Part 2*. Louisville, KY: Westminster John Knox, 2004.

———. *The Day the Revolution Began: Reconsidering the Meaning of Jesus's Crucifixion*. San Francisco: HarperOne, 2016.

About the Author

Jed Brumfield is a Pastor, Theologian, and Author whose mission is to proclaim the message of the Kingdom of God and to help believers live as God's dwelling place in the world. He is the founder and lead pastor of Ascend Life Church in Louisiana and the visionary behind the Ascend Kingdom Learning Institute, a ministry dedicated to equipping the body of Christ through biblical teaching, theological formation, and practical discipleship.

Jed earned his Bachelor of Arts in Ministry and Leadership from Oral Roberts University and is currently pursuing a Master's degree in Christian Ministry at ORU. His theological studies and pastoral training have equipped him to bridge academic rigor with practical ministry, combining deep biblical insight with a passion for real-world transformation.

He is the author of *Kingdom Identity: Living in God's Image and Likeness* and *FaithFuel: 365 Daily Devotionals to Ignite Your Spirit*. His forthcoming book, *The Garden of Light (Children's Book)*, reflects his ongoing desire to provide tools that inspire believers toward intentional, daily growth in Christ.

With a heart for scholarship and shepherding, Jed seeks to challenge, encourage, and equip pastors, students, and believers to embrace their calling as Spirit-filled witnesses of the Kingdom. He is especially passionate about teaching the continuity of God's presence—from Eden to the New Jerusalem—and reminding the Church that His dwelling is both a present reality and a future hope.

Jed lives in Louisiana with his wife, Sha'Myra, and their two children, Caleb and Jaed. Together, they are committed to building a Christ-centered legacy rooted in love, faith, and Kingdom purpose.

For ministry inquiries, speaking engagements, or to connect further, email Jed at:

Email: info@jedbrumfield.com

YouTube: @OfficialJedBrumfield

Facebook: Jed Brumfield

Other Works by Jed Brumfield

- Kingdom Identity: Living in God's Image and Likeness
- FaithFuel: 365 Daily Devotionals to Ignite Your Spirit

www.ingramcontent.com/pod-product-compliance
Lightning Source LLC
Chambersburg PA
CBHW021615120626
46545CB00001B/233